EDUCATION AND BIODIVERSITY

EDUCATION
AND
BIODIVERSITY

By

Dr. M. Lakshmi Narasaiah
M.A., Ph.D.

Professor of Economics
Co-ordinator, Dept. of M.B.A. and Commerce
Special Officer
Sri Krishnadevaraya University Post-graduate Centre
Kurnool–518 002
Andhra Pradesh
(India)

DISCOVERY PUBLISHING HOUSE PVT. LTD.
NEW DELHI-110 002

Published by:
Tilak Wasan

DISCOVERY PUBLISHING HOUSE PVT. LTD.
4383/4B, Ansari Road, Darya Ganj
New Delhi-110 002 (India)
Phone : +91-11-23279245, 23253475, 43596065
E-mail : discoverypublishinghouse@gmail.com
sales@discoverypublishinggroup.com
web : www.discoverypublishinggroup.com

Edition: **2020**

ISBN: 978-81-8356-307-9

Education and Biodiversity

Printed at:
Infinity Imaging Systems
Delhi

Preface

As human population has surged this century, the populations of numerous other species have tumbled, many to the point of extinction. Indeed, we live amid the greatest extinction of plant and animal life since the dinosaurs disappeared some 65 million years ago, with species losses at 100 to 1,000 times the natural rate. But humans are not just witnesses to a rare historic event, we are actually its cause. The leading sources of today's species loss, habitat alteration, invasions by exotic species, pollution, and overhunting are all a function of human activities.

Human activities have pushed the percentage of mammals, amphibians, land fish that are in "immediate danger" of extinction into double digits. The principal cause of species extinction is habitat loss—the result of encroachment by humans for settlements, for agriculture, or to claim resources such as timber. A particularly productive but vulnerable habitat is found in coastal areas, home to 60 per cent of the world's population. Coastal wetlands nurture two thirds of all commercially caught fish, for example. And coral reefs have the second highest concentration of biodiversity in the world, after tropical rainforests. But human encroachment and pollution are degrading these areas: roughly half of the world's salt marshes and mangrove swamps have been eliminated or radically altered, and two thirds of the world's coral reefs have been degraded, 10 per cent of them "beyond recognition".

Dr. M. Lakshmi Narasaiah

Contents

1

Wanted
A New Deal for the Universities

Higher education must meet new demands in order to turn out well-trained professionals instead of unemployed graduate. We are living through a period of profound historical change, marked by an on-going knowledge revolution. Society is changing far more quickly than the structures it has created and the universities are lagging behind these changes. They, and the educational system in general, continue to teach the use of static processes, forecasting models based on historical experience and the memorizing of solutions to already solved problems.

Higher education systems in both North and South are in crisis, both quantitatively and qualitatively. Naturally the developing countries are the hardest hit, both in terms of available resources and levels of student enrolment.

Is the crisis due to a shortage of funds alone? Does the fact that the countries of the North invest ten times more per student than those of the South mean that graduates from the former are ten times better trained? Common sense says yes. But in most cases the answer is no. Generally speaking, university education has failings all over the world, in some cases because it is an offspring of a wasteful society, indifferent to the resources with which that society provides them.

The Missing Link between Education and the World of Work

In the United States, for example, many teachers and researches come from developing societies which should theoretically have given them a less sound training than that provided by the immense academic and financial resources of the United States system. But this is not the case: they compete professionally and scientifically, with no major problems. In many areas the results of university training are comparable.

Professionals move around because they need jobs and want to work in the best possible working conditions. There are, for example, almost 30,000 African Ph.Ds working in Europe and North America, and thousands of Latin American and Asian professionals working in the Untied States. By the beginning of the 1990s about a million professionals had emigrated to the developed countries over the previous three decades, and the figure has increased considerably in the last five years. While the number of opportunities and access to them are uneven, there is little difference between North and South as regards quality; nor is the availability of funding the only basis for improving the system.

The problem is that post-secondary training today is diploma-driven. It is based on rigid study programmes and is changing at a rate which takes little or no account of the speed of knowledge accumulation. This is despite the fact that today's graduate professional needs to have followed a flexible curriculum and must be a problem solver, extremely adaptable to new processes and technologies, generously endowed with creativity and firmly inclined towards lifelong learning, as is clear from the studies on skilled labour done by industrialized countries and from numerous OECD studies.

A recent study of the relationship between higher education and the labour market observes that there appears to be no connexion between the increase in professionals' level of knowledge and changes on the labour market. Although the market undoubtedly demands basic skills and knowledge, it is attaching increasing importance to the emotional and psychological attitudes of future employees.

Although post-secondary education is clearly associated with higher personal incomes, lower unemployment and greater opportunities to climb the social ladder, unemployment rates for people with higher education qualifications continue to be high in both North and South. Graduates unemployment in Europe, for example, varies between 1.4 per cent and 16.6 per cent depending on the country. What's more, many graduates are working in jobs outside their field of training. The increase in graduate unemployment in the developing countries is largely due to the drastic fall in demand from the major employer of graduates—the state—as a result of international competition and new political and economic approaches. The private sector is in no position to absorb the supply of surplus graduates. World Bank studies carried out in Asia, the Middle East, North Africa and certain Latin American countries show that graduate employment is increasing.

All the same, higher education cannot be held wholly responsible for graduate unemployment nor for the correlation that should exist between training, study programmes and demand for labour. It is often said that higher education is failing to provide training in the activities required by the market, but the market is often incapable of adequately anticipating the type of professionals it is going to need.

A survey conducted in Florida (USA) among multinationals in the high-tech and services sectors reveled companies that were unable to identify the professional qualities that would be required within ten years and, in many cases, within five years. This is not surprising, in view of the spectacular rise of the internet between 1994 and 1998 which caught many hardware and software firms unawares. It is in information technology that redundancies and high unemployment levels are occurring, because systems are constantly changing and because of strategic mergers between the major companies.

Another example of the difficulty of making reliable predictions concerns those made by the European Community and the US Government regarding the type of jobs that would be needed at the beginning of the new century. These predictions were inaccurate: what had been forecast to occur after 2001 actually came about in the late 1980s and early 1990s.

It can be said, however, that professional training over the coming years will focus on areas such as high-tech electronics, information technology, aqua-culture, agro-energy, biotechnology and energy physics. Jobs in information and communication systems will require new qualifications which will have to be continually updated. The service sector will experience spectacular growth in the field of leisure and recreation because of the reduction in working hours. New professions in the human sciences such as "ludicadology", incorporating psychology, pedagogy, information science and the technology of education, play and creativity programmes, will replace the old single-discipline approach.

In short, the great occupational change looming ahead will call for increased interdisciplinary, revitalisation of the disciplines related to thick and aesthetics and sweeping changes in the attitudes of teachers and students: for the professional of the future, education will be a lifelong process, and education and work will go hand in hand.

The great challenge will thus be to create a stable relationship between higher education and society through strategic alliances with the production system designed to promote participation by all sectors of the economy in the university's basic and applied research programmes and by production-sector specialists in university teaching.

The problems of the university are also those of society, and so are the responsibilities. This rises the question of the university's specific culture, especially the teacher-student relationship. Planning is currently based above all on the teaching staff, which is more corporatist than academic. Physical spaces, salary scales, curricula, structures and timetables are more closely geared to the needs of the teacher than of teaching. This is the case all over the world.

More serious still, this teacher-centred culture is giving way to one that is even more dangerous for the survival of university education: an administration-centred culture. This would mean an education system dominated by bureaucrats and the kind of management structures which would place an institution whose function is to produce and disseminate knowledge on the same footing as a detergent factory or a multinational travel agency.

But no strategy for change can work unless higher education adapts to the challenge of the knowledge explosion. It is vital that course content should be geared to what learners "must know" and not to what teachers "know" or "think they know". This will force teachers into a permanent renal of theories, techniques and processes, keeping up with knowledge produced both inside and outside the university. Higher education is evolving towards a model in which lecturers and students will be permanent learners and where curricula will be drawn up on the basis of innovation, fresh knowledge and the latest teaching and learning technologies. Above all the university must teach people to think to use common sense and to give free rein to the creative imagination.

❍ ❍ ❍

2

Wiring up the Ivory Towers

Prestigious universities are forging alliances to conquer a share of the e-learning market and stand up to virtual competitors. Just like airline companies, universities around the world are forming partnerships and consortia in response to the pressures of globalisation. The World Education Market held in Vancouver was a timely sign: the fair, expressly organised to foster relations between universities, training providers, software companies and representatives from nations with large education needs attracted participants from over 60 countries.

This race to "partner up" is fuelled by a number of factors. In most industrialised countries, government funding for higher education has decreased, forcing institutions to look for new markets either to subsidize campus programmes or just to remain viable. There is a growing need for lifelong learning as "jobs for life" vanish and the information society drastically reduces the shelf-life of almost any educational qualification. Technological developments, increasingly necessary for learners in all fields to master, offer ever more innovative tools for supporting e-learning.

For business, online learning is "the" new market opportunity with the need for re-training and professional updating predicted to increase a $11.5 billion industry by 2003. Business is better able to develop and maintain the technological infrastructure necessary to run large online systems and everyone, including the universities, recognizes that it takes robust telecommunications technology to deliver education and training on the scale demanded.

A host of companies has sprung up to help universities shape and package courses for online presentation, while network providers are jockeying for position to deliver online education.

The United States is the undisputed leader in the field, prompting governments in the U.K., Canada and Australia to commission being eroded by U.S. ventures turned global Canada and the U.K. are in the early stages of setting up their own virtual universities. But what has become clear is that the conservative and labyrinthine decision-making processes which characterize most university procedures are being jolted by a race to get a share of the lifelong learning market.

So far, the most common approach for universities to break into the e-learning universe has been to develop courses specifically for a corporate partner or to form alliances among themselves. Universities 21, a company incorporated in the U.K. is a network of 18 leading universities in ten countries.

Very often, prestigious universities has stayed clear of going fully online, seeing a danger to their brand name. Many are limiting their offerings to continuing education programmes and/or non-degree courses, and more often than not, they are aiming at the corporate market. One Company UNext.com, has partnered with first-class institutions such as the University of Columbia (U.S.) and the London School of Economics to create online courses marketed under the name Cardean University. Their target: the Fortune 500 companies as well as individual adults. They've managed to attract Noble laureates to design courses and the universities have formed spin-off for-profit companies specifically to develop online programmes. This facilities the commercialisation of software and other products, and is a way to take a commercial approach to continuing and professional studies without compromising the Univesity's standing.

Then there are the free-standing for profit virtual universities which are arousing the ire of institutions that have prided themselves on a long history of public service. The most quoted examplar is Phoenix University, the largest private outfit in the U.S. Now owned by the Apollo Group, it operates the country's largest online programme with 12,200 students. The university tracks students progress and contacts those who don't submit assignments on time or fail to enrol in subsequent courses. Many critics question Phoenix's blatant commercialisation, but few doubt the university's impact on continuing professional development provision.

Although e-learning is in its infancy, its impact can already by gauged. New providers are coming on the market all the time and the trend is accelerating to the point of upsetting universities virtual monopoly in educational accreditation. An Information Technology training course offered or accredited by Microsoft has undoubtedly become more valuable than a Bachelor of Science from a renowned university.

The more consumerist the approach of the education provider, the more what is taught is influenced by demand. MBAs dominate e-learning provision and IT courses are a close second. While the new consumer/learner demands flexibility, choice and just-in-time learning opportunities, suppliers will inevitably arise who are focused on meeting the demand at the expense of quality and value. And is the consumer really the best judge of what course material to choose? Education is a more complex "product" than toothpaste or washing powder. A totally consumer driven education market is unlikely to be in society's best interest in the long term. The commercialisation of education usually goes hand-in-hand with desegregation: course design, delivery, tutoring assessment and accreditation may be carried out by different organisations. Students might study courses or modules from different universities or providers and then put themselves forward for examination and accreditation by yet another institution. While most academics loathe marking assignments, they regard this scenario with horror, and blame commercialisation for the demise of the 'community of scholars' concept of a university. The death of the 'course' has also been predicted, with learners—especially corporate and on-the job learners—demanding short study modules. What then happens to the ability to get an overview of a field when learning consists of the students selecting a whole series of unconnected learning "bites"? Learners will be "zapping" between short sequences or presentations much as they do between television channels.

But while some faculty view e-learning with alarm, technology-based learning is where most of the pedagogical innovation is taking place in universities. Multimedia learning resources and interactive simulations are being developed for the web. Collaborative learning activities, new forms of online assessment and small group teaching technologies are making online courses more stimulating, interactive and attractive than many face-to-face taught courses.

Despite "doom and gloom scenarios", most moderate observers of the scene see a continued future for the campus university, especially at the undergraduate level, while e-learning will above all cater to adult professional and independent learners. Some commercialisation of education is good if it fosters innovation, concern for quality and responsiveness to consumer demands. But if some is good, more is not necessarily better! Not in education at least.

❍ ❍ ❍

3

Biodiversity

As human population has surged this century, the populations of numerous other species have tumbled, many to the point of extinction. Indeed, we live amid the greatest extinction of plant and animal life since the dinosaurs disappeared some 65 million years ago, with species losses at 100 to 1,000 times the natural rate. But humans are not just witnesses to a rare historic event, we are actually its cause. The leading sources of today's species loss, habitat alteration, invasions by exotic species, pollution, and overhunting are all a function of human activities.

Human activities have pushed the percentage of mammals, amphibians, land fish that are in "immediate danger" of extinction into double digits. The principal cause of species extinction is habitat loss—the result of encroachment by humans for settlements, for agriculture, or to claim resources such as timber. A particularly productive but vulnerable habitat is found in coastal areas, home to 60 per cent of the world's population. Coastal wetlands nurture two thirds of all commercially caught fish, for example. And coral reefs have the second highest concentration of biodiversity in the world, after tropical rainforests. But human encroachment and pollution are degrading these areas: roughly half of the world's salt marshes and mangrove swamps have been eliminated or radically altered, and two thirds of the world's coral reefs have been degraded, 10 per cent of them "beyond recognition". As coastal migration continues—coastal dwellers could account for 75 per cent of world population within 30 years—the pressures on these productive habitats will likely increase".

Habitat loss tends to accelerate with an increase in a country's population density. This is bad news for the world's biodiversity hotspots-species-rich ecosystems at greatest risk of destruction. Twenty-four of these hotspots, containing half of the planet's species, have been identified globally. Some of the most important hotspot countries will reach population densities that have been linked with very high rates of habitat loss. Five of the six most biologically rich countries could see more than two thirds of their original habitat destroyed by 2050 if this historical relationship holds.

Related to loss of habitat is the growing incidence of plant, animal, insect, and microbial invasions of ecosystems worldwide as human interchange increases. These "exotic species" sometimes dominate local ecosystems, eliminating native species and reducing overall diversity. Exotics are implicated in 68 per cent of all fish exticntions in the United States this century, for example. Growth in human travel and commerce explains many accidental invasions by exotics, but foreign species are also deliberately introduced into farms, plantation forests, and aquaculture systems. Although only 1 per cent of exotics cause widespread damage, exotic species are the second leading cause, after habitat destruction, of species loss worldwide.

Other, often diffuse effects of expanded human activities also disrupt ecosystems. Nitrogen, for example, is now made available to plants at more than twice the preindustrial rate as a result of fertilizer production, cultivation of nitrogen-fixing crops, and the burning of fossil fuels. This overfertilisation of the Earth favours some species at the expense of others, leading to a reduction in diversity and resiliency of land and aquatic ecosystems.

Likewise, greenhouse gas emissions could disrupt ecosystems on a vast scale. As with nitrogen, increased levels of atmospheric carbon may favour some species over others: annuals over perennials, for example, or deciduous trees over evergreens. To the extent that greenhouse gases induce changes in global climate, many species may be at risk as habitats shift or shrink, and as some life forms, such as insects or animals, adapt and migrate more quickly than others, such as plants. And as sea levels rise with a change in climate, ecosystems such as coastal wetlands could be destroyed.

4

Climate Change and Human Health

Changes in the India's climate, stemming from the greenhouse effect, are highly likely to damage human health. Food and fresh water supplies will be disrupted, millions of people displaced, and disease patterns altered dangerously and unpredictably.

Human health could be affected by even quite small changes in average mean temperature, and there is the prospect of some major diseases flourishing in warmer conditions and of more resistant strains of infection emerging.

The population in India most vulnerable to the negative impacts of global warming are in the lower-income groups, residents of coastal lowlands and islands, those living in semi-arid lands, and the urban poor in the squatter settlements, slums and shanty-towns of large cities.

Present strategies for immunisation, coping with disease vectors or carriers, providing safe drinking water, and improving nutrition are all based on existing climate regimes, ecosystems, and sea and solar radiation levels. These are all expected to change, but exactly how much cannot be predicted. It is therefore, virtually impossible to adjust health and nutritional strategies to take account of possible climate changes.

Humans can adapt to moderate changes in temperature and to occasional extremes. But this adaptive capacity is relatively low in infants and the elderly; it rises through childhood and adolescence to reach a maximum which can be maintained up to about 30 years of age.

A changing climate would alter the ecosystems of the vectors or agents which carry or cause many diseases, whether these be viruses, bacteria, parasites, plants, insects or other animals such as mosquitoes and snails. As the weather warms, the boundaries of the tropics may extend into the present subtropics, and parts of temperate areas may become subtropical. As air temperature increase, some diseases will become common in regions which once rarely knew them and where there is little natural resistance to them. As a result, death rates may also climb significantly.

It is possible that warmer weather around the world will cause increases in summer diseases and decreases in those associated with winter. Diseases contracted from both water and air will also spread more readily as ambient temperature rise. In a warmer climate, mosquitoes and other vectors also may migrate vertically up into highlands which were once too cold for them. This may be particularly hazardous in tropical highland areas where there is no natural resistance to malaria.

Changes in temperature, rainfall, humidity and storm patterns may affect diseases borne by vectors in two ways. First, they will directly affect the vector's reproduction rate, biting rate, and the duration and frequency of human exposure. Second, they may modify agricultural systems or plant species, thus changing the relationship between host and vector. Development rates of malarial mosquitoes, for example, increase with warmer temperatures, but these pests need wet areas in which to breed.

Sea-level rise could also spread infectious diseases by flooding sewerage and sanitation systems in coastal cities, and increase the incidence of diarrhoea in children. The flooding of hazardous waste dumps and sanitation systems could lead to long-term contamination of crop lands.

Rising seas may also disrupt marine habitats land aquatic food chains. Since fish constitute 40 per cent of all animal protein consumed by the people of India such a disruption of the marine ecosystem would affect the food supplies of many millions of people and dramatically increase protein deficiency and malnutrition. Changes in the availability of food and water, as well as radical shifts in disease patterns, could initiate large migrations of people, exacerbating food shortages, overcrowding, social stress and instability.

Some of the factors contributing significantly to global warming, such as the burning of fossil fuels and the use of chlorofluorocarbons (CFCs) and halons, threaten human health in other ways too. A typical petrol-driven motor car, for example, emits carbon monoxide, sulphur and nitrogen oxides, hydrocarbons, low-level ozone and lead—all of which are hazardous to health.

The ozone-depleting CFCs and halons pose a particular threat to humans through an increased risk of skin cancer, cataracts and lower immunity to other illnesses as a result of increased exposure to ultraviolet B radiation from the sun. Skin cancer risks are expected to rise most among fair-skinned.

5

Population Growth and Climate Change

Over the last half-century, carbon emissions from fossil fuel burning expanded at nearly twice the rate of population, boosting atmospheric concentrations of carbon dioxide, the principal greenhouse gas, by 30 per cent over preindustrial levels. All major scientific bodies acknowledge the likelihood that climate change due to the build-up of greenhouse gases in the atmosphere is indeed under way. The 15 warmest years on record have all occurred since 1979, and 1998.

The destabilisation of our climate threatens more intense heat waves, more severe droughts and floods, more destructive storms, and more extensive forest fires. The related shifts in rainfall and temperature may jeopardize food production, the Earth's biological diversity, and entire ecosystems, as well as human health by expanding the ranges of tropical diseases. Unless efforts to curb them are stepped up, carbon emissions will continue to grow faster than population over the next 50 years, driving the Earth's climate system into unchartered territory. The Intergovernmental Panel on Climate Change (IPCC) estimates that an eventual two-thirds reduction in global emissions is needed to avoid precariously high levels of atmosphere carbon dioxide concentrations.

The IPCC and U.S. Department of Energy (DOE) project that emissions from developing countries will nearly quadruple over the next half-century, while those from industrial nations will increase by 30 per cent. Although annual emissions from industrial countries are currently twice as high as from developing ones, the latter are on target to eclipse the industrial world by 2020.

Higher per capita carbon emissions accounts for roughly 55 per cent of the increase in emissions projected for developing nations. Emissions per person are due to more than double from 0.51 tons of carbon per year in 2000—just one-fifth of the industrial level—to 1.14 tons in 2050. The remaining 45 per cent of emissions increases is due to population growth.

Fossil fuel use accounts for roughly three quarters of world carbon emissions. As a result, regional growth in carbon emissions tend to occur where economic activity, and related energy use, is projected to grow most rapidly. Emissions in China are projected to grow over three times faster than population in the next half-century, as emissions per person soar from 0.77 tons of carbon to 2.81 tons due to booming economy that is heavily reliant on coal and other carbon-rich energy sources. In Africa, in contrast, emissions per person are expected to scarcely change—growing from the current level of 0.33 tons in 2050, despite a three-fold increase in total emissions.

The effects of population growth are most profound in countries where people are heavily emitters. For example, the 115 million people added to the population of the United States between 1950 and 1998—an increase of nearly 75 per cent in just 45 years—account for more than one-tenth of current global emissions. And the carbon emissions of the 75 million people who will be added to the U.S. population in the next 50 years roughly equal the emissions of the 1.3 billion people who will be added to Africa during that period.

Deforestation and other land use changes account for the remainder of world carbon emissions. Forests have served as a sink for carbon throughout much of human history. In recent years, however, the world's forests have become net sources of atmospheric carbon, largely due to forest burning and clearing in the tropics. Six months of fires in Asia in 1997 and 1998 released more carbon than Western Europe emits from fossil fuel burning in an entire year. The carbon contribution from this source will likely increase in coming years as the burgeoning human population continues to cut down forests.

6

Urbanisation and the Environment

Is abandoning the cities the answer to the growing ecological problems of urbanisation? The trend at any rate is in the opposite direction. At the beginning of this century, only every 10th person worldwide was a city dweller. At its end, more than half the global population will be urbanites. And most of the urban population growth will take place in the developing countries, led by Asia.

Compared to other parts of the world, however, the urbanisation process in Asia is currently not even particularly far out in front. Worldwide, city dwellers account for 43 per cent of the total population. Industrial nations have an average urbanisation rate of 72 per cent. Less industrialised countries have 34 per cent. In the Asia-Pacific region the rate is 30 per cent, in Latin America 72 per cent, and in Africa 33 per cent. The urbanisation growth rate in a number of Asian countries has in fact slowed compared with earlier years. Nevertheless, not only industrialisation, but also the increasing degree of urbanisation has emerged as a growing burden on the environment in many Asian countries.

Changed Urbanisation Pattern in India

Environment burdens are just as much a problem in the old industrial nations as they are in India. But each group has a specific pattern of development. The urbanisation process in India has proven to be more pollution-intensive than that in the old industrial nations of Europe and North America. There are several reasons for that:

- industrialisation in India is restricted to a few locations which are often concentrated in and around capital cities. Although environmental damage continues to be minor at a national level, these locations have higher pollution levels than those ever reached in industrial nations;
- furthermore, besides the strong regionalisation of industries, the industrialisation pattern of India shows a great diversity of environmental hazards. The trend to establish "last industries first", which is promoted by progressive industrialisation, leads to a country producing certain dangerous materials before they have been covered by state regulations;
- the time factor has to be seen as an important element in the emergence of these already highly regionalised environmental burdens. In India industrialisation and its concomitant urbanisation is taking place within a ban population grew tremendously.

Growing Environmental Damage

Water pollution in India is caused mainly by domestic sewage. For example, households are responsible for 75 per cent of the pollution of the rivers. The domestic sewage problem got more and more out of control with growing urban populations. Pipe-based waste water systems are rare in this country. In India dealing with waste has an extremely low priority. The type of waste disposal depends mostly on what the cities can afford. The present level of air pollution is also very high.

Innovative Approaches to Solutions

Environmental protection and economic development are seen as contradictions. Economic development can only be achieved at the cost of higher levels of environmental pollution. And in reverse, if pollution is to be controlled and reduced this can only be done to the disadvantage of further development. In the meantime, however, numerous instances of successful urban environmental management are developing. They could help to change and subsequently break through the existing pattern of thinking. The following approaches can be viewed as important.

Combining regulations with incentives: The introduction of lead-free petrol and the mandatory equipping of new cars with catalytic converters is still by no means common in India. As numerous cars without catalytic converters are still able to use lead-free. Converters were then at first made compulsory for higher-powered cars, and later also for compact models.

Combining regulations with simple controls: Apart from general limitation of the number of cars in the city, its most important single measure to prevent traffic jams and the additional petrol consumption and pollutant emissions caused by them.

High economic growth in India has in fact led to a general reduction of poverty. But the distribution of income, particularly between urban and rural areas, has remained relatively constant. Urban environmental and traffic problems have increased heavily during the same period. These developments can be attributed to a certain pattern of official action (or "non-action"):

- governments have made efforts in supplying roads, but neglected the demand for mobility;
- governments are preoccupied with supplying water, and have neglected follow up problems, above all the questions of waste water disposal and treatment. In Indian cities, for example, this leads to the absurd situation that due to the mushroom like growth of the cities and the increased water pollution linked with it, water must be brought in over ever greater distances and at ever greater expense;

- governments take a one-sided look at noxious substances. Concentrations of harmful substances in water and in the air are in fact checked, and some measures are taken against individual pollutants of single sectors (e.g. lead emissions by the transport sector).

But an integrated policy which operates integrated environmental management with the aim of comprehensively relieving the burdens on the environment has not yet been developed anywhere. To consider such a concept, it is necessary to cut loose from the customary way of approaching problems. It makes sense not to separate the problem areas from each other according to sectors and pollutants, but rather on the basis of their ecological impact.

Orienting on demand hits the core of the concept of ecological modernisation, which is about reducing the intensity of resource use (note, at this stage this does not yet mean the absolute reduction of inputs). At the same time, sights are set on a lower use of land with the same size of population, or also lower energy consumption with the same degree of added value or the same per capita income.

Finally, the importance of governments for creating framework conditions must be emphasised once again. Because the actors come from different spheres, such conditions are essential.

From the time of the Greek polis, it was the ambition of the Greek city councillors to pass on a city that was more beautiful than the one they had taken over. There is a long way to go before such an attribute asserts itself in India (and elsewhere).

7

Sustainable Cities

Today almost one half of the world's population lives in cities. The world's cities are growing by one million people each week. Cities today play a significant role in development. They continue to attract migrants from rural areas because they enable people to advance socially and economically. Cities offer significant economies of scale in the provision of jobs, housing and services, and are important centres of productivity and social development.

However, the stress of this rapid urban population growth is often overwhelming. The long list of afflictions includes urban poverty rates of up to 60 per cent. Despite growing investments, more than one-third of the urban population live in substandard housing. Forty per cent of urban dwellers do not have access to safe drinking water or adequate sanitation. Primarily due to a rapid growth and a deteriorating urban environment, at least 600 million people in human settlements (cities, towns and villages) already live in health and life threatening situations, and almost 50 per cent of these are children.

The high rate of urban population growth in most regions has led to common problems: congestion, lack of funds to provide basic services, a shortage of adequate housing and declining infrastructure, to name a few.

While these problems are occurring in urban areas, cities still have an important role to play in protecting the global environment in the face of rapid urban population growth. Agricultural and livestock production in rural areas are pushing farther and farther into ecologically fragile regions and cannot support growing population. The finite land and water resources make it imperative that human settlements be carefully planned. Indeed, sustainable urbanisation will ease the pressures caused by encroachment on fragile natural habitats.

India's cities offer a bewildering sight to any visitor: the congestion caused by rapid population growth and a continuing rural-urban drift often leads to conditions which defy all rules of orders, hygiene and environmental safety. Inadequate leadership, corruption and mismanagement have a harmful effect on the physical, environmental, social and ethical structures of cities in India.

Millions of people live in inadequate conditions—without piped water, electricity, security of land tenure, access to roads or health facilities. The means available for production and financing of housing and urban infrastructure are too limited to meet basic needs.

Reducing Poverty and Creating Jobs

Urban poverty is rising at an alarming pace, especially among women. The informal economic sector—which makes a substantial contribution to the delivery of services, production of goods, building of infrastructure and housing construction—often provides the only opportunity for the urban poor to make a living.

Local informal housing construction, for example, generates up to 20 per cent more jobs than high-cost construction. Street hawking, waste recycling and food production are primary sources of income among the urban poor and are illustrative of the creativity of survival strategies.

However, the informal sector itself is often highly exploitative and fails to raise people's economic development beyond mere subsistence. Larger economic strategies and more participatory urban planning approaches that take stock of local skills, technologies and materials are required to generate new and better-paying job opportunities in cities and towns.

Incorporating Environmental Concerns

In 1992 the Rio Conference on Environment and Development designed the Agenda 21 Programme of Action to help save a planet endangered by environmental neglect and plagued by poverty and underdevelopment. Most of the goals agreed to in Rio can become reality only through local action in cities where environmental threats are increasing. Again, it is the urban poor who are particularly endangered by environmental degradation and pollution. The world's Agenda 21 will fail if the city's environmental agenda (population, inadequate sanitation, water supply and waste management) is not addressed. This is being recognized by local authorities all over the world.

Sustainable development in the twenty first century will to a large degree, depend upon how cities, towns and villages everywhere interact with the environment and utilize natural resources.

Increasing Awareness of Gender Issues

Women and men use and experience cities differently, according to their roles, responsibilities and access to resources. For example, when basic services are lacking in a settlement, more often than not it is women who take on responsibilities such as water collection and refuse disposal. Women often have unequal access to resources such as property, credit, training and technology. All of these factors must be addressed urgently, as they make it harder for women to improve their living standards and those of their children.

Disaster Mitigation Relief and Reconstruction

As cities become large and more densely populated, they become increasingly vulnerable to natural and man-made disasters such as earthquake, floods, industrial hazards, epidemics, civil strife and wars. Poor people are forced to live in the most exposed, dangerous and cramped conditions; in flood-prone areas, on steep hillsides or near polluted streams and waste dumps. As a result, they are most likely to lose their homes or their lives when disasters occur. Better planning, access to affordable urban land, and improved construction methods can reduce the extent of catastrophes.

These successful and sustainable approaches to poverty eradication; managing the urban environment; providing access to land, shelter and finance; empowering women and men; and many other issues will have to be documented and disseminated widely.

8

Ecotourism or Ecocide?

Ecotourism is the fastest growing part of the world travel business, but whether it destroys more than it protects will depend upon how it is put into practice.

For the travel and tourism industry, ecotourism is the fastest growing 'market segment', generally equated with nature tourism. Interpreted merely as a product, however, it may be ecologically based but not ecologically sound, responsible for sustainable.

To incorporate these vital characteristics ecotourism must adhere to three essential principles: The first is, perhaps, the most obvious. As an industry based on the beauty and diversity of nature, it is evident that it should not deplete or degrade those resources and thus prejudice its own future. Ecotourism must, therefore, be ecologically sound, requiring a two-way link between itself and environmental conservation.

To consider nature without recognising the link with people will, however, compromise sustainability. It is now widely recognised that conservation cannot be divorced from development issues. The second principle is therefore that ecotourism must be responsible, paying regard to local needs and improving local welfare.

However, to be truly sustainable, ecotourism needs to fulfill the ambitions and expectations of all interests. The third principle, then, is to consider not only the interests of tourism enterprises and organisations, but also visitor satisfaction, the needs of tourists.

If, ecotourism embodies these essential principles, symbiotic relationships between the varying interests should follow, with environmental protection resulting both from and in enhanced standards of living for local populations, continued profits for the tourism industry, sustained visitor attraction, and revenue for conservation. An examination of ecotourism across these dimensions, highlights not only its potential but also its problems.

Local Benefits

The high ground claimed by ecotourism, in terms of its contribution to development, is that, in principle, it offers enhanced prospects for local involvement compared with conventional tourism. As well a moral obligation to incorporate the local people in projects that affect them, such incorporation has important developmental implications.

Tourism income may be captured locally through revenue sharing schemes, through entrepreneurship and labour, and through the sale of tourist merchandise. Tourism can also act as a catalyst, and even provide some of the finance, for the improvement of essential services such as clean water, sanitation, electricity supply and transport. It may also provide an incentive for improved education and skills and the potential for participation in decision making.

Local involvement also makes sense for conserving natural environments. It has been recognised that, as people realise the benefits from ecotourism, support for conservation increases. Ecotourism may also provide the incentive for the survival of a traditional culture. The cultural and the natural are often inextricably linked to form the composite attraction of a particular ecotourism destination. The terracing of the Himalayan foothills, the hot springs at Tatopani, Sikkim are all examples of the fusion of the natural and the cultural.

Greater local involvement makes practical sense for national and local governments, agencies and operators using local labour, expertise and knowledge. Education is a two-way process, improved understanding of local circumstances is likely to increase project efficiency. Building upon local experience and traditions provides a foundation for wise and successful development, and, simultaneously, an ecotourism asset.

Introduction to indigenous uses of natural products also broadens the base of environmental interpretation. Local involvement is not without its problems, however. Revenue sharing schemes may neither benefit the most needy, nor those most adversely affected. Beneficiaries may often be passive recipients, rather than active participants. The emphasis must be on participation rather than patronisation, if traditional livelihood are removed they must be replaced with others.

Local participation, however, often consists of employment rather than entrepreneurship, where constraints of costs of entry, language, education and skills operate. Furthermore, the nature of local employment tends to be low skilled, poorly paid and often seasonal. The higher status, better paid jobs, particularly managerial positions, tend to be occupied by outsiders.

Industry Profits

The integrity of the tourism 'product' is vital to the interests of tourism entrepreneurs, and all those who are associated with them, such as tourist boards, government departments, NGO's and international aid agencies. Tourism operators benefit from public support, increased credibility and demand for associated products. Sound environmental practice often makes good business sense.

There are, however, many practical and institutional obstacles to effective ecotourism management, not the least of which will be the problems of vested interests who are more concerned with short term profits than with the long-term.

Pressure of Numbers

Another dilemma is the sheer problem of numbers. To confine attention, however, to the consideration of small-scale, more easily managed ecotourism projects, involving small specialist groups paying high prices, is to invite ecocide at higher levels.

Rapid growth rates imply inevitable change. Psychological carrying capacity (as well as other types of carrying capacity) will probably be breached and visitor satisfaction compromised. This is especially true when visitors are concentrated in space and time.

However much a principled definition of ecotourism is advocated, it must be recognised that so-called ecotourists are not an homogeneous group. The spectrum of participants embraces hard-core nature tourists through to casual day visitors. Their behaviour and consequent impact will vary accordingly. It is essential, therefore, to attempt to match numbers and types of ecotourists with destination characteristics.

Paying for Conservation

Willingness-to-pay surveys of ecotourists across the globe show a consistent response of $10 as reasonable visitor's fee. Certain unique sites, or those harbouring more charismatic species, can support higher fees. The potential revenue for conservation is therefore evident, but often not realised.

Where the fee falls below the amount visitors are willing to pay, the capability to contribute more fully towards conservation remains latent. It is also necessary to ensure that a proportion of revenues accrues locally. Percentages of revenues directed towards conservation vary between sites. Often high proportions end up in central treasuries.

The Challenge

The major role players in ecotourism all have a stake in its sustainable development. Their present and future interests are, in many ways, tied to one another. Given the multitude, and diversity, of stakeholders a completely sustainable outcome is, however, likely to remain elusive.

The grand challenge is to reconcile sometimes complementary, but often conflicting interests. The essential dilemma is to balance demands of ever-increasing 'new-tourists' escaping from the confines and pressures of urban life, and reacting against the characteristics of mass tourism with the needs of the environment, the aspirations of tourism organisations, and, most importantly, the basic needs of the local population.

Although a win-win scenario, where all interests gain, is the ideal outcome, there will often be situations where one interest may gain at the expense of another. National Parks, for example, may bring benefits for conservation and for visitors, but the local population is likely to lose out if they are excluded from their traditional activities.

The situation is fraught with discontinuities. A win situation for one interest in a particular place at a specific point in time is likely to be a loss for another. It is necessary, therefore, to recognise conflicts and identify relative costs and benefits. Arriving at the most sustainable outcome is likely to involve trade-offs. It is unlikely to be optimal either environmentally or developmentally, but, in the circumstances, it will be the most feasible and most practical. And, hopefully, ecocide will be circumvented.

10

Water
An Educational and Informative Approach

The most characteristic element of our planet is undoubtedly water. Indeed, more than two-thirds of the earth's surface is covered by water—the total volume representing almost 1,500 million cubic kilometers. About 94 per cent of this water is found in the oceans, almost 6 per cent is located underground and in glaciers whereas rivers, lakes, soil moisture and atmospheric vapour, which constitute the major source of drinking water, account for a mere 0.0221 per cent of the total volume.

Water is indispensable for all living organisms. Life, as we know it, is impossible without water. It is present in all aspects of our life—directly or indirectly next to the air we breathe and together with the soil that we live upon, water constitutes the most important part of our environment, our most precious resource. And yet, except in the arid or semi-arid regions of the world, its value is generally overlooked until some catastrophe—natural or man-induced—forces our attention to its worth. But even so, no sooner is the situation remedied than, more often that not, we revert to our old attitude.

The reason for this sort of indifference is undoubtedly attributable to the fact that, except in exceptional circumstances, water has always been considered as a "gift of the gods", as some thing that human beings are as naturally entitled to as the air they breathe. Its supply, however uneven, water resources used by humanity. A supply of drinking water and sanitation in urban centres are crucial for preserving human health.

For some decades it has been known that the misuse of water resources is responsible for many important environment problems. For example, in many industrialized cities both surface water and ground water are seriously contaminated. This deterioration is a consequence of a range of human activities, sometimes in isolation, others over a large area or a long period of time. Among examples of the latter is modern agriculture, whether it uses irrigation or not, as a result of the intensive use made of mineral fertilizers and pesticides.

Water Shortage: Exaggeration, Reality or Bad Management?

Some of these problems have made news and have created the impression that water shortage will be one of humanity's big problems in the coming decades. Sometimes this feeling is due to genuinely manipulative publicity campaigns to justify the setting in motion of hydraulic mega projects which basically benefit a few large construction companies. The truth is that except for a handful of very specific cases, no problems of water shortage are to be found almost anywhere. On the other hand, cases of bad water management are not rare at all.

Basic Principles for Good Water Management

Good management of water resources—and of almost all other natural resources—must be based on the principles of solidarity, "subsidiarity" and participation. The physical reality requires that these resources be considered a common heritage of humanity both now and in the future. By "subsidiarity" we mean that water management should be as decentralized as possible: what one person or any minor social group can do should not be done by a higher authority. For example, what local government can do should not be done by a regional, state or central government. Participation consists in water users playing as large a part as possible in decisions affecting water, in keeping with each state's or country's social and cultural structure. Obviously this participation calls for a certain cultural and technical knowledge—a hydrological education—on the part of those users.

The need for participation by users is even greater in the exploitation of groundwater. In this case, users tend to extract water independently of one another. They often fail to realize, until there is a serious economic or environmental impact, that their pumping affects other people who rely on the same water supply as has happened.

Water shortage is rarely a serious problem: in fact, in some cases the problem is exaggerated to justify the construction of large works using taxpayer's money. On the other hand, the contamination of surface and groundwater tends to be a problem which rarely receives adequate treatment. Successful water management should be based on three basic principles: solidarity, subsidiarity and participation. The specific way in which these principles are applied will vary from one state or country to another, but the effectiveness of water management will depend in large measure on the hydrological education of the general public.

The universal way of obtaining freshwater is from rain. River systems are the results of the excess water that falls on dry land in the form of rain. On the one hand, rainwater penetrates the permeable soils, saturates them and accumulates to form groundwater reservoirs, or aquifers, which can come to the surface in the form of springs. On the other hand, the water is absorbed by vegetation, which uses it for pumping minerals and then evaporates it by transpiration. Some rainwater is lost because it evaporates immediately on falling on impermeable surfaces like the asphalt of roads and cities. Running water courses finally flow over saturated soils, shaping the complex systems of the watersheds or river basins.

Since each basin's natural system has developed gradually and has grown up according to the yearly distribution and fluctuations of rainfall, we have to appreciate that any large-scale project for redistributing water by means of pipes, as if it were gas or electricity, is a journey into the unknown. This is because it destroys the results of the work of shaping the climate, however transitory it might be.

Variable Volumes

All water supplies are of variable volume. Both the discharge of rivers and the level of lakes and aquifers depend on rainfall. As these resources are components of a larger system, the river basin, a reasonable policy would be to manage water resources according to the characteristics of each basin. This would require, first of all, a proper understanding of the system so as to adapt use and consumption to the existing supply. Conserving river systems as much as possible in their natural state is the best guarantee for the preservation of the landscape and of a constant supply. Grondwater reservoirs aren't canals, but are more like lakes, so that pollution leads to the build-up of a debt which is paid in years to come.

Consumption

Water consumption has increased in recent years as a result of not only population growth but also an increase in living standards. In the rural areas the introduction of new farming methods, the spread of irrigation and the excessive use of fertilizers and pesticides causes very high consumption—it is estimated that more than 2/3 of water consumption is used in irrigation. Agricultural pollution also endangers both surface water and aquifers, which receive water full of chemical products. Many cases of eutrophication, the enrichment of water by nutrients that accelerate the growth of algae, derive from the run-off of fertilizers. The practice of intensive stock-raising on farms with large numbers of animals also brings about these problems of over consumption and pollution. Cleaning the stockyards requires large amounts of water which is then released into the environment with high concentrations of nitrogen.

As for industries, they have in the past taken little care over water consumption and dumping, and in many areas the need for proper attention comes as something new. The best thing would be to make industry take its water at a point down-river from where it returns it or, better still, generalise the use of closed circuit systems based on the constant recycling and reusing of the same water.

As regards human consumption, the general attitude to cleanliness is based on diluting pollutants. One example is the success of the use of the Water Closet which involves diluting a few decilitre of urine in 10 or more litres of drinking water: quite a record in wastefulness.

Another aspect to be considered is the different quality of the water that falls on well formed soils from the water that falls on roads, cities, airports, suburbs and built-up areas and whose composition is less stable and "worse" than that resulting from a more uniform interaction with mature soils. Remember that streets, roofs, communication routes, airports and built-up areas already cover a high proportion of the earth's land area and are still on the increase.

Purification techniques should be based especially on the natural processes that include biological activity. Otherwise—for example, if physico-chemical methods are used—there can be side-effects such as an excess of mud or sediments. The strategy to follow is to optimize operations in our use of water according to the discharge and to the distribution of contamination. A system in the form of a conduit or channel, such as a river, can respond relatively quickly. On the other hand, lakes and dams can only do so up to a point, because they show more inertia and irreversibility and take longer to clean.

Large lakes, not to mention the sea, might seem a good place to dump contaminating refuse, but they can't then be cleaned. This is the price we pass on the future generations: a comfortable attitude, but an unacceptable one.

9

Fresh Water and the Environment

It is widely recognized that water is going to be one of the major issues confronting humanity at the turn of the century and beyond. We are facing a crisis as regards the quantity and quality of water supply, but we have yet to experience the full social and political impact of that crisis. The escalation in the population and the quest for continued development is leading to conflicting pressures on water resources. Such resources are the ultimate recipient of pollution from various socio-economic activities associated with urbanisation, agriculture, mining and clearing of native vegetation. Pollution originating from human waste, especially where appropriate sanitation facilities are not available, or are located too close to water supply sources affects both surface water and ground water.

This makes water supply and health perhaps the most important issue for the large proportion of the global population. Paradoxically, the demands for "sustainable management" and increasing global population require more potable water from a declining available potable water base.

It is universally accepted that proper water administration is a critical component of sustainable development—that is, development that meets the needs of both present and future generations. Indeed, water is an essential factor in a large number of productive activities, of which one of the most important is the production of food by irrigation. This activity, accounts for two-thirds of the has always seemed inexhaustible because water has a natural regenerative cycle which, until the present century, was beyond human control or interference—or even proper comprehension. But the trend of social, political and economic evolution, notably in the past 200 years, with an increase of industry, agriculture, technology, and above all, a vertiginous population growth, as led to a dramatic revision of the age-old belief that no demands made by human populations on the natural resources of the planet are in the process of setting in motion vicious circles in the environment from which it is becoming increasingly difficult to extricate ourselves, not only as concerns the present, but far more important, for the future. Thus, the overuse—or abuse—of water resources has started affecting seriously not only the water cycle but the very nature of water in such a way that, in conjunction with other abuses of the environment, the results have been climate changes, droughts, flooding, desertification on the one hand and acid rain, water pollution and eutrophication on the other.

Actually, the problem of water is to be considered less in terms of quantity—though with a steeply increasing world population making increasingly heavier demands on a fixed quantity of water, one will sooner or later be confronted with this aspect of the problem too—than in terms of proper distribution of available resources taking into account sound management, stock-age and maintenance of quality. For among the major preoccupations of humanity in the coming years, adequate supply of freshwater to the teeming populations figures in the forefront. Between 1900 and 2000 water consumption will have globally increased ten-fold and though the share of agriculture, the major consumer of fresh water, is expected to drop significantly (from 90 per cent to 62 per cent approximately), that of industry and the cities will have increased enormously (approximately, from 6 per cent to 24 per cent and 3 per cent to 8 per cent respectively).

Given the current trend of societal evolution i.e. greater emphasis on industry and increasing migration towards the cities added to the global population boom, these figures are certainly cause for concern. Not only because of the damages caused to freshwater resources through the increasing use of fertilizers in the search to maximize agricultural production to cater to the increasing populations, but equally because the mushrooming of industries and urban concentrations are sources of increasing water pollution. Though the industrialised nations have more than their fair share of blame in this matter insofar as the current state of water pollution goes, for the future, it is in the developing world that lies the major source of concern. Lack of resources for adequate urban planning, the increasing role of industry in the search for economic solutions added to uncontrollable population pressures are already on the way to creating an explosive situation in a great number of developing nations with the available water supply becoming more and more inadequate in terms of quantity as well as quality. And then one considers the fact that around 80 per cent of all diseases are estimated to be water related, and that by the year 2000, 51 per cent of the world population will be urban based, one can hardly be accused of exaggeration in speaking of an explosive situation.

Attacking such a vast problem is no mean task. Water being at the very source of life, what concerns water concerns every aspect of life. Thus, be it climate change, pollution, desertification, deforestation, food production....or whatever other major environmental problem that humanity is confronted with today, water constitutes one of the prime factors. Managing our water resources with care and intelligence for the use of present and future generations is a major responsibility which has to be shared by governments and the public alike, for no sector alone can deal efficiently with so vital a problem which affects not only the present but also the future of humanity. Again, as in the case of biodiversity and climate change, the problem of water being a global problem, international cooperation is of utmost importance since activities in one part of the planet are likely to produce consequences in other regions of the world. Concerted action by the international community alone is capable of dealing effectively with a problem of such far-reaching consequences.

If our planet is to be saved from disaster—for in jeopardising our water resources we are guilty of nothing less than condemning life itself on our planet—we have to work for sustainable results: short-term plans for the present which will dovetail into medium-term ones for the coming generations without compromising the possibility, at the same time, of careful long-term planning to guarantee the future of the planet. In this, the part of environmental education and information of the people is fundamental. No strategy, no policy, no plan—be it ever so well prepared and implemented—can hope to succeed without the active and effective participation of the main actors—the people who must be properly educated and informed. For this age-old techniques, beliefs—mentalities must be brought in line with present day realities. People have to learn to think differently in order to veer from a course which, however right in the past, has been shown to be less than adequate for present conditions—and catastrophic for the future—and must therefore needs be altered.

Changing mentalities is neither an easy nor a rapid process. It is difficult to go back upon the accumulated experience of generations—even in the face of stark realities and scientific evidence. Moreover, when dealing with such global and fundamental issues as water, where even "scientific evidence" tends to be stated in tentative terms, the task becomes more onerous. Add to this the fact that the problem presents itself most presently in developing countries which are equally subject to enormous economic pressures which tend to reduce the cope of possible solutions. We are thus faced with the enormous task of trying to change attitudes, values, mentalities of populations whose geographical, socio-cultural and economic conditions have already fashioned priorities other than those that would precisely permit them to overcome their difficulties in a sustainable manner. In other words, of persuading people of abandon traditional short-term strategies in favour of perhaps more unattractive but eventually sustainable, long-term practices.

A veritable Herculean labour—which can only be accomplished through information and education. And in particular, through environmental education and information whose avowed aim is precisely to develop the understanding, knowledge, skills and motivations leading to the acquisition of attitudes, values and mentalities which are necessary to deal effectively with environmental issues and problems. Sound and systematic environmental education of the people associated with concerted local, national and international action, is the only means to finding a sustainable solution to this problem. The ground has to be paved through adequate information on the subject followed by educative processes adapted to specific local conditions. For a uniform education, whether formal or non-formal, might perhaps do more harm than good as its rejection, due to its unsuitability in the light of local customs, beliefs, traditions... might only serve to reinforce the very attitudes that it seeks to change. In each region, each country, each locality the educative processes must correspond to the socio-cultural, historical, economic conditions of the people. Only then can we hope to arrive at the change in mentalities around the planet which, coupled with consistent, parallel support from national and international institutions, will lead to the safeguard of what is perhaps our most precious resource—Water.

11

Sustainable Tourism Development

Tourism has grown into one of the world's major industries and has thus also become an increasingly important, if complex, issue for environmental policy. Unless it is developed in a sustainable manner, we will be unable to achieve key objectives of global environmental policy such as the preservation of biological diversity, the prevention of climate change or the conservation of natural resources.

Tourism itself depends a lot on the existence of unspoilt nature and landscapes, as well as a healthy environment. If nature is plundered, landscapes are destroyed or water, energy and soil resources are over-exploited, the economic basis of tourism is also undermined. The needs of tourism do therefore overlap with those of environmental protection and nature conservation.

On the one hand, for instance, tourists are becoming increasingly environmentally conscious and are looking to get back to nature and enjoy unspoilt environments when on holiday. On the other hand, however, the number of international tourists is growing constantly. The proportion of long-haul journeys is also increasing steadily, especially in the industrialised nations, where travel is now taken for granted as part of people's lifestyles and has become an important factor in social status. The many different types of travel and holidays are covering more and more countries and regions and, as a result, increasing numbers of previously unspoilt natural environments are being opened up to tourism. This applies equally to coastlines, small islands, coral reefs, rock formations and mountain regions.

There is growing recognition of the need for tourism to develop in a sustainable and environmentally friendly manner. Many countries have, for instance, introduced regulations which require environmental impact surveys to be carried out at least for larger tourist developments. Since the Rio Summit in 1992, there have also been more initiatives in support of sustainable tourism at international level:

- Sustainable tourism allows for the rational use of biological diversity and can contribute to the preservation of that diversity;
- The development of tourism must be controlled and carefully managed so that it remains sustainable;
- Particular attention must be paid to tourism in ecologically and culturally sensitive areas, where mass tourism should be avoided;
- All parties concerned, including in particular the private sector, have a part to play in bringing about the sustainable development of tourism, and voluntary initiatives (codes of conduct, quality labels) should be encouraged;
- Particular importance should be attached to the local level, which is not only responsible for the sustainable development of tourism but should also derive particular benefit from tourism.

It will mark the successful beginning of internationally co-ordinated efforts to make tourism environmentally and socially sustainable so that many generations to come, can continue to experience and enjoy the beauty of nature on our planet.

❍❍❍

12

Children's Health and the Environment

Children today live in an environment vastly different from that of a few generations ago. Economic development, increased urbanisation and the consequences of war in many countries have added to the traditional environmental hazards, those problems associated with environmental pollution. Thus, while some traditional children' diseases such as diarrhoea, malnutrition and infectious diseases persist in many countries, environmentally-related illnesses such as asthma, respiratory illnesses due to environmental tobacco smoke (ETS), as well as mortality and morbidity due to injuries, are increasing. In childhood cancer in some countries and the potential risks of endocrine-disrupting chemicals are among the emerging health threats that need careful vigilance. Children of lower socio-economic status are likely to suffer disproportionately from all these health threats as a consequence of living in highly polluted environments, poor quality housing, lower levels of education, and of restricted access to environmental and health care services.

Children's Vulnerability

The concern for children's vulnerability to environmental health threats is based on several factors. Children receive greater exposures than adults do because they drink more water, eat more food and have higher breathing rates per unit of body weight. Because they are undergoing rapid growth and development, toxicant effects at specific times may have irreversible consequences. For example, if vital connections between nerve cells fail to form during brain development, there is high risk that the resulting neuro-behavioral dysfunction will be permanent and irreversible. Also, because most children have more future years of life than adults, they have more time to develop any chronic disease that may be triggered by early environmental exposures.

Public Health Threats

Asthma, injuries, and the effects of environmental tobacco smoke (ETS) are among the most significant public health threats to children. Childhood asthma is increasingly prevalent in almost all countries. What causes asthma is not known, but several environmental factors, such as indoor air quality (particularly exposure to the house-dust mite) and ETS, have been linked with the increase in asthma. In addition, outdoor air pollutants such as particulates; sulphur dioxide and ozone can exacerbate asthma symptoms. ETS, especially smoking by the mother, is a known risk factor for asthma. ETS is also known to cause acute and chronic middle ear disease and is associated with sudden infant death syndrome (SIDS).

Potential for Prevention

The variation in asthma and injury rates and the evidence of the role of certain environmental factors underline the potential for prevention. Public policies should seek to avoid preventable childhood diseases by preventing exposures to environmental agents and considering children's characteristics and susceptibilities in the development of environmental health legislation. Promoting citizen awareness and participation in policy-making through education and access to environmental information are important elements in achieving a safe environment for children. In this context, children are not only consumers with rights, but also citizens who can play an active role towards their own protection.

International Awareness

Several international agreements have acknowledged children's vulnerabilities and have committed their signatories to protect children's health from the effects of a deteriorating environment. This year, many countries will address several of the environmental health threats to children through international and national action. It is expected that a large international collaborative initiative will result under the guidance of WHO and other international organisations.

13

Sustainable Tourism and the Environment

Tourism is high on the international agenda. The 7th session of the Commission on Sustainable Development focused on tourism and subsequently work programmes on sustainable tourism are being developed. Also the Convention on Biological Diversity is embarking on tourism programmes and bilateral and multilateral financial institutions placed tourism high on their priority lists. The UN declared 2002 as the International Year of Ecotourism and the World Tourism Organisation adopted a Global Code of Ethics for Tourism at its General Assembly, held in Santiago de Chile.

The World Tourism Organisation forecasts that there will be 702 million international arrivals in the year 2002, that arrivals will top 1 billion in the year 2010 and that by 2020 international arrivals will reach 1.6 billion—nearly three times the number of international trips made in 1996, which was 592 million.

Travellers of the 21st century will go farther and farther. The 'Tourism 2020 Vision' forecast predicts that by 2020 one out of every three trips will be a long haul journey to another region of the world. It is expected that China will become a major force in international tourism and the WTO predicts that about 100 million Chinese will take international trips by 2020, thus putting them in fourth place in numbers of travellers after Germany, Japan and the United States. By the same time, China will attract 137 million visitors—63.5 million overseas visitors travelled to

China in 1998 and thus outrank France as the world's top destination. It is estimated that during 1999 France will receive a record number of tourists of more than 70 million; in 2007 France hopes to attract 90 million visitors. The key resource for the most popular tourist destinations is the natural environment: coastal resorts, tropical rainforests, wildlife in national parks and alpine skiresorts, all rely on a mixture of natural beauty, good weather and safe conditions to attract holiday destination is landscape and natural environment, followed by climate, the cost of the journey and the historical features of the place to visit, hence, conserving the ecological integrity and environment is imperative if tourism is to be sustained.

The pressure from millions of tourists on water and marine resources, on land and landscape, on wildlife and habitat is enormous and often has devastating impact on the environment and the local population who are increasingly deprived of access to clean water and other natural resources.

In some regions, particularly in small island countries, tourism is one of the major reasons for wasting and polluting water: on average one tourist consumes at least 6 times more water than a local resident.

Major water wasters and polluters are golf courses. In many countries, golf has brought heavy ecological and social costs: deforestation, the destruction of bio-diversity and erosion; dispossession of peoples' homes and farms; over-consumption and pollution of water and very high use of pesticides and fertilisers which threaten local residents, workers, wildlife and the golfers themselves. A survey by the Japanese National Doctors Health Insurance Association has revealed that many golfers, caddies and residents living near a golf course suffer from skin inflammation, disorders of the ear, nose and throat and other respiratory illnesses to the inhalation of pesticides because up to 90 per cent of the chemicals sprayed on golf courses end up in the air. In some areas in Thailand, diseases emerged which, prior to the construction of golf courses, had not been known.

In some regions, golf courses have depleted water supply, agricultural production has come to a halt, peasants have become impoverished and forced to migrate to urban areas in search of employment. Golf courses take large amounts of land. It is estimated that each year world wide up to 5,000 hectares of forest are cut to clear land for golf courses.

Very often, the construction of golf courses forms an integral part of a comprehensive tourism project. Adjacent to the golf course condominiums and/or hotels are built, very often also a marina, an airport and a casino. Studies have shown that such a complex not only has touristic objective but is often connected to drug trafficking and money-laundering. Even the US State Department has emphasised the link between tourism, money-laundering and offshore banking.

Cruise ships are a major cause for pollution in the Caribbean, destroying maritime life and reefs by releasing waste into the ocean. Recently the Royal Caribbean, the world's second largest cruise line was fined a record sum of US $18 million for dumping waste oil and hazardous chemicals into the sea. The company admitted to routinely dumping wasted oil from its fleet and that it deliberately dumped in U.S. harbours and coastal areas many other types of pollutants, including hazardous chemicals from photo processing equipment, dry cleaning shops and printing presses. Some hazardous materials, including toxic solvents from dry cleaning operations, were illegally placed in the garbage aboard the ships. The material was then either incinerated on the ship or dumped in U.S. or foreign ports mixed with ordinary garbage.

It was announced that the Royal Caribbean Cruise reported a profit of US $338 million in 1997, a 93 per cent increase over the previous year, Carnival Corporation's

Holland, the biggest cruise company with a turnover of US $3 billion in 1997 made a net profit of US $836 million, 25 per cent more than in 1996. Both cruise companies have recently been fined millions of dollars for dumping untreated bilge water, oil and other waste into Alaskan waters.

However, the impact of oil and hazardous waste on water, maritime life and coral reefs is devastating and all fines paid for the damage caused by the cruise ships will not revive dead corals.

A recent Green peace study on coral reefs—one of the marine world's great natural treasures—predicts that the coral bleaching which dramatically whitened many of the world's reefs last year will escalate rapidly under accepted global climate models and that the damage would wreak havoc in fisheries and tourism, disrupting the economies of many nations.

A WWF study recently published on "Climate Change and its Impacts on Tourism", warned that droughts, rising seas, flash floods, forest fires and diseases could turn profitable destinations into holiday horror stories. The report urges the tourist industry to persuade western industrialised governments to take more concerted action to reduce their nations' carbon dioxide emissions the main cause of global warming.

The Need for Action and Education

If governments, the international community and the tourism industry want to save the world's major tourist destinations, immediate action is required. Governments and the tourism industry must abide to the principle that environmental protection is an integral part of tourism development. In order to protect the environment and mitigate the damages caused by tourism, some countries have decided to take action: The Spanish Island Minorca and the Seychelles will introduce Eco-tax on tourism. This tax will be around US $ 12 per person in Minorca and its revenues are earmarked for the maintenance of national parks and the restoration of damaged coastline. Visitors to the Seychelles will have to buy a so-called "gold-card" at a price of 100 $ which entitles unlimited access to the country; income from this card will be used for sewage management and protection of fresh water supply.

Only if tourism investors and developers:

(a) consider the natural capacity for the regeneration and future productivity of natural resources;

(b) recognise the contribution that people and communities, customs and life styles make to the tourism experience and therefore accept that these people must have an equitable share in the economic benefits of tourism; and

(c) listen to local people in the tourist destinations, tourism may become sustainable.

Education and awareness raising campaigns at all levels are therefore imperative.

14

Crime or Development

Cutting Crime Rates is Essential for Sustainable Development

Crime is increasing almost everywhere in the world. The cost of crime prevention and criminal justice is crippling for many developing countries. Crime scares away investors and undermines the confidence of the people in the organs of the state. But to effectively control crime, social and economic conditions must improve.

Freedom from crime, safety from violence at home and on the street, public safety and the means to make cities safer are essential ingredients of sustainable development. To feel safe from crime is as important to a person as access to food, shelter, education and health.

Available data suggest that crime is increasing all over the world. Robbery, burglary and other interpersonal crimes are believed to have doubled or tripled in industralised countries over the past 30 years. In many other countries, rapid economic and political transition has been associated with a similar escalation of crime rates in a single decade. Urban areas are the worst affected: today, more than half the world's population living in cities of more than 100,000 people are victims of a crime at least once every five years. As more and more of the world's people leave the countryside for the city, crime rates seem locked into an inexorable upward spiral.

The level and type of crime are the result of a range of local, national and regional factors, including traditional culture and belief, political and economic stability, the quality of policing, and the availability of guns and other weapons. In Sao Paolo, for example, a major contributor to the 2,000 annual homicides in the early 1990s was the killing of more than 1,000 suspects per year by the police itself. In the Indian state of Maharashtra, and in Bangladesh, bride-burning and wife-murders account for many of the large number of homicides.

Fear and Reality

But perception of crime may be out of proportion with reality. People commonly believe their society is more violent today than ever before. However, many countries of the North were more violent during the early years of industralisation. Increasing fear of crime, therefore, is not linked in any simple way to growth in actual levels of crime and frequently continues to increase even when crime rates themselves decline. Analysts believe that this accelerating fear of crime is fuelled by ever-faster global communications and greater exposure of crime in the media. The wide spread perception that crime is out of control can be just as damaging to a country's ability to attract investment as actual levels of crime. Social and political stability are further casualities.

Crime and Development

Development has to be delivered to eliminate the socio-economic triggers of violence; but the delivery itself often triggers violence. However, it is not clear whether development is directly or indirectly linked to crime. Does the development process itself trigger crime, or should the blame fall on the inequality that development often brings about? Many argue that it is the very lack of development that causes crime. There is current research to support either position.

It seems to be certain, though, that urbanisation, rapid liberalisation of the economy, political upheaval, violent conflict and inadequate policing are among the many and complex factors—often linked to poverty and inequality—contributing to growing levels of crime.

The mushrooming growth of cities is a global phenomenon. Urbanisation uproots and dislocates communities and creates new inequalities between haves and have-nots. At the same time, traditional value systems and structures that once served to restrict criminal behaviour are undermined. People become isolated, alienated and less constrained by social norms. As the rural populations of Asia, Latin America and Africa pour into the cities, semi-legal shanty towns appear and grow to accommodate them. Life for hundres of millions of rural migrants means no security of tenure, and little or no work and illegality can soon become their only option.

Cities in the South also have a predominantly young population especially young men—who are every where the main perpetrators of crime. Violent conflict as in many Third World countries is another factor leading to an explosion of crime. It uproots and destroys communities, deprives people of their livelihoods, take young men away from their families and habituates them to violence, rape and killing. Perhaps above all, it saturates a society with guns.

Structural adjustment programmes of World Bank in developing countries which have led to increasing unemployment and cuts of government spending on education and health programmes, have also contributed to rising crime levels. Liberalisation of trade, increased foreign investments, and a rise in international tourism have led to city streets full of expensive foreign cars and shops full of imported luxury goods—a provocative slight for those marginalised by such reforms. Satellite TV which brings the lure of the affluent society even into the shanty towns of the poor is seen as another factor promoting crime and lawlessness.

As governments that have tried to "crackdown on crime" have discovered raising the level of policing alone seldom produces the desired reduction in crime rates. A sustained reduction is more likely to result from a policing strategy that addresses the underlying causes of lawlessness, rooted in urban deprivation and inequality. Nevertheless, public confidence in the police and their effectiveness is acting against crime rates. An effective police force is large, adequately paid and highly trained, ideals that are beyond the reach of many cities of the South. As a result, the police is corrupt in many countries. For instance, government estimates suggest that 70 per cent or more of all police personnel are involved in some form of corruption, ranging from bribetaking to cocaine-trafficking. They derive a significant proportion of their income by extortion from motorists. Many of the problems of corruption can be linked to low pay, low morale and lack of trust in the police force.

The Cost of Crime

Although crime rates are high and increasing worldwide, the cost is disproportionally crippling to countries of the South. Fighting crime can impose a terrible drain on the financial resources of the poorer countries. The global economic cost of urban violence amounts to trillions of US dollars. Crime does not only victimse the individual, but can also destroy communities, ruin businesses and empty state coffers. In the United States alone, the cost of urban crime in 1993 was estimated at $ 425 billion. In South Africa, the cost of crime was more than $7 billion or 18 per cent of the national budget for 1996/97. Crime and violence are draining resources from families, households, business and government. These costs are completely unsustainable in a developing economy.

High levels of crime scare away foreign tourists and are discouraging both foreign investment and development aid. Crime nurturs an atmosphere of violence, social insecurity and economic stability and deters companies, governments and aid agencies alike. Companies that do set up in cities with high crime rates have to budget specially for the potential cost of theft or damage, or the need to hire extra protection against them. They also have to pay premium salaries to their foreign staff to compensate them for 'hardship posts'. Often, however, companies rather avoid cities where the lives of their staff is in danger. A high level of corruption also tends to work against foreign investment, because it increases transaction costs. Likewise it contributes to lower aid levels as 'donor fatigue' increases when public money is siphoned away from development projects into private pockets.

Dangers to Democracy

Crime also exacts a political cost. Fear and insecurity from crime prompt demands for swift and ruthless action by law enforcement agencies. Governments may seize the opportunity to strengthen a state's repressive apparatus, eroding civil rights by targeting dissidents or political opponents as well as criminals. Where people have no confidence in the state's ability to protect them from crime, alternative forms of crime control, ranging from private security firms to vigilantes and death squads, can emerge. Even worse, the inability of an elected government to control crime is frequently cited as part of the 'justification' for the military to step in and seize power. All too often, the price paid for high levels of crime includes a tragic diminution of democracy and human rights.

Breaking Crime's Stranglehold

Governments, law enforcers, NGOs and development agencies increasingly accept that reducing crime is essential if the countries of the South are to have sustainable development. Criminal justice systems modelled on those of the wealthy countries of the North may be inappropriate for dealing with the problems of developing countries. New forms of cheap, decentralised justice need to promoted, stressing prevention and involving communities. Such systems already exist in some countries.

In the long term, however, crime prevention is inseparable from social development. Violence and crime are usually the result of inequality and poverty, and they certainly breed fastest in a society characterised by extremes of inequality and social exclusion. Ultimately, only measures that protect communities from deprivation, joblessness, injustice and insecurity will also make them safer from crime.

15

Innovative Milieus—Cities

Cities provide the local bases for international linkages. This is where the virtual worlds of highly specified communication networks are anchored. Complicating matters, globalisation and urbanisation have certain features in common. They challenge the existing order, constantly frustrate planning and emphasise plurality. Tension is the norm, cannot be avoided, and must, therefore, be handled constructively. Not coincidentally, however, cities posses civilising qualities: their very existence depends on reducing levels of violence.

Globalisation and urbanisation are two trends characterising the present. These two phenomena are closely linked because globalisation means that global networks emerge, which have their nodes in cities. The networks are heterogeneous, frequently based on competition and provide the stuff of which conflicts are made. At stake are cash flows, transnational companies, international civil society, migrant groups, religious communities, multilateral politics and cultural interdependencies. Nor should one forget the challenges of organised transnational crime or global terrorism. This is where global interests seek to maximize profits, but also where local grassroots and civil society develop new claims to assert rights to liveable urban space.

Global Cities

Global cities are defined as locations, which support international networking. They are under particular pressure and it sometimes even seems doubtful whether a global city can be treated as a single, coherent entity at all. There is a prevailing trend towards fragmentation because of the permanent competition of various norms and values, identities and social realities. This trend is exacerbated when populations organise in various local networks. On the other hand, the global networks use virtual habitats with far-reaching rules of largely homogenous quality. In this sense, financial markets, for example, command their own virtual cities—as do heroin or cocaine dealing. Such virtual contexts, are, in turn, locally embedded in real cities. They dominate some neighbourhood but hardly affect others.

The traditional concept of "world cities" is passe. The notion referred to command centres with transnational significance and cosmopolitan culture. However, the hierarchy of various urban functions is no longer stable or permanent. Whereas the world city was viewed as control centre of the modern world system, the global city is integrated in distinctive global networks, none of which can automatically be assumed to be dominant, structuring or even yielding to the national government. Rather, we are dealing with distinct realities which are compatible only to various degrees and sometimes even incompatible. Global cities are characterised by confusion, because their various realities can no longer be integrated into a single system.

Global cities, moreover, contribute to our planet's environmental crisis. The size of airports is a good indicator of how global any particular agglomeration has become. On the other hand, air travel is a major, unregulated source of green house emissions. Petrochemical fuels, on which most cities thrive, are the world market's core commodity.

In addition, large urban agglomerations are often located on the most fertile land and thus there extension reduces agricultural production. Every urban centre depends on food from outside, stimulating not only traffic but also intensive production in the hinterland, which in turn, has also become international. Afterall the pineapples on display in Frankfurt's supermarkets do not grow in Germany, nor can the citizens of Toronto consume domestically produced lemons and oranges. It must be considered, however, how sustainability of natural resources would be challenged, if instead of population concentrations, we had highly overpopulated rural region in need of adequate infrastructure.

Cities have always served diverse cultures as arenas for encounter and exchange and accordingly, also as arenas of conflict. This applies to contemporary global cities more than ever before. Nevertheless, they are more than just articulation nodes of transnational networks. In view of the fact that the world is divided into territorial states, cities also belong to national political systems, for which they normally play distinct and decisive roles. Fashion, trends and other types of societal change have always originated from cities. Modern representative democracy was born of the cities—key historical events such as the Storming of the Bastille and the Boston Tea Party provide the evidence. On the other hand, state institutions are based in cities, from the national tax administration to judicial authority. A further aspect is social stratification, because a nation's elite usually lives in the major cities.

Of course, not all of a city's people and communities are integrated in global networks. Social contexts with specific local histories, which different from the realizations of global networks, are equally relevant. In the cities local, national and' global phenomena inter-relate. Executive managers with worldwide spheres of activity depend on their maids who—particularly, but not only, in poor countries—may hardly ever leave the household.

Traditionally, the urbanisation debate revolved around the experience of those nations that industrialised early. Empirical research normally looks at the aglomerations in Europe, North America and Japan, where the respective histories have national characteristics. In contrast, the development of Singapore, Kuala Lumpur or Jakarta resulted from colonialism. The dynamism of their growth was, from the outset, associated with global networks.

To this day, Third World Cities tend to be much more diverse than most OECD cities. While nationalism served as a central mechanism to integrate the urban populations in Europe in the 19th century, similar efforts in the colonial cities were regarded as a threat and suppressed as effectively as possible. Consequently, it is still common to find urban cultures in which rural places of origin define identities. People relate to their "homeland", which may be thousands of kilometres away and which some may not visit in their lifetime, rather than with the immediate neighbours they meet everyday.

All cities have their own history resulting in particular features. Urbanistion becomes specific in each city, but is likely to also affect other regions, because cities never exist in isolation. They always belong to systems of various corresponding centres, because population groups pursue the same interests, or, at least, related interests. This typically is expressed in architecture, with the result that, even today, one can still find traces of the Northern Italian Renaissance in small towns of other countries.

Moreover, urbanisation implies a civilising process. To exist in the long term, cities must curb violence, despite the diverse nature of their populations and their conflicting interests. Wherever that is not done successfully, cities become irrelevant fast. The connection between civilising and urbanism is based on two pillars. These are firstly the public sphere and political deliberation and, secondly, something I have described elsewhere as "locality". Locality ensures social control through personal contacts and interlinking institutions. It is not about communities or districts, but networks of relationships which are integrated through various activities. Locality arises from initiative and self organisation and can hardly be orchestrated by administrations. Locality and public sphere complement each other. Otherwise, selfcreated and self-regulated interactions could not persist under the pressure of real estate speculation, official town planning, and other dominant societal forces.

The World Bank holds a similar view. Its urban peace programme zeroes in on strategies to reduce violence. The focus is on supporting local communities in an effort to increase "social capital". In a similar vein, violence erodes social capital, as it reduces trust and cooperation within formal and informal social organisations that are critical for a society to function.

Planning Paralysis

The rapid growth of many cities makes building social capital particularly important. There must be scope for creative and cooperative improvisation, because local authorities are often strikingly overburdened. The enormous size of mega-cities with several million inhabitants makes it clear that comprehensive control and even planning are impossible. In many cases, civil servants do not even notice that new slums have formed within a few years, which may easily have more inhabitants than large towns. Such developments make the demand for better planning obsolete from the outset. Too often, we do not really know what makes mega-cities tick.

It is clear that private enterprise steps in where profits are attractive. This applies to local business but also to multinational corporations. Well-known examples are provided in the construction industry, building homes, offices, factories and roads. But schools and hospitals are also operated privately. Without private bus, and in some places, even rail companies, traffic would collapse completely. Lucrative mobile telephone markets are expanding, where the conventional fixed line telephone network has been overburdened for decades. Electricity and water supply offer opportunities, both for multinational companies smelling profit and for slum dwellers attempting to tap utility services for free.

It is not uncommon for clashes to occur with city authorities. What official regulations demand often makes little sense to the firm engaged or the people affected. Influential persons are often involved in the private companies, which helps to avoid official rules or to have them re-written. Whether corruption takes place or formal decision processes are adhered to, may make surprisingly little difference on the ground. Typically very little attention is paid to the needs of poor people.

Nevertheless, urban life offers opportunities for economic, political and cultural participation even for marginalised people. This is what leads to rural-urban migration in the first place. Admittedly, it also means tough competition for housing space. There is ever-increasing demand for shelter. At the same time, the public and private sector are neither interested in, nor in a position to fulfill the right to an 'adequate shelter. The poor urban population can improve its fate only in the slums and often only using its own initiative—such as through locally supported micro-finance schemes to get legal access to land.

This kind of societal creativity in initiative and self-organisation is not limited to the production of housing. It is also visible in petty trading and the informal sector, which blossom in economic niches and continues to discover new niches. Among the fields of activity are waste recycling, domestic services or, of course, drug peddling, "Innovative milieus" are not only found in business high-rises, universities and research institutes. They are also prolific in slums markets and even on garbage dumps.

Initiative, self-organisation and social creativity have political consequences. Communal self-determination and the building up of local organisations depend on democratic principles. Formal participation is relevant—but so is scope for informal improvisation. The relevance of grassroots activity is one reason for totalitarian and authoritarian regimes always looking at cities with great scepticism.

Revolts and protest movements normally start in the urban centres. How political challenges are dealt with, on the other hand, sets precedents, which define what is normal and to be expected. This is institution building in practical terms. It happens spontaneously and unplanned-with long term consequences far beyond the city limits. Periods of rapid growth, moreover, are particularly critical because they are, by definition, times of rapid change.

Conclusion

Things often happen in unplanned and disorderly ways in cities and agglomerations. Especially in poor countries, the living conditions are often anything but idylic. Nevertheless, there is no alternative in the development process but to build on this difficult foundation. Inspite of all the dirt, misery and hardship, urban environments offer prospects not only of survival but also of participation, democratic modernisation and civilisation (in the basic sense of reducing violent interaction). That people are flocking into the cities proves that these places attractive in spite of their dismal slums, overflowing drains and congested traffic. It is telling that it is so rare, in poor countries, to see anyone return to their rural homes for good.

Globalisation accelerates the dynamics described above, while urbanisation is, at the same time providing the base for making international networks ever more important. Both trends are interrelated. They imply that city life is gaining relevance in economic, political and cultural terms with the influence of specific urban settings potentially spreading far beyond the borders of the nation-state, without, however, making urbanisation more predictable or even more amendable to planning. On the contrary: the potential for conflict is growing.

❍ ❍ ❍

16

Assessing the Costs, Benefits, and Risks of GM Crops

Opponents of genetic engineering in agriculture consider it the work of the devil, claiming it harbours untold ecological risks and health hazards and make farmers worldwide dependent on a small number of seed producers. Its advocates, however, see genetically modified crops as a way out of poverty, a unique opportunity to produce enough food for the world's growing population. This paper tries to assess the pros and cons of GM crops case-by-case. The world's farmers already produce enough food to meet global needs and that hunger is due largely to patch patterns of food distribution and lack of purchasing power. The task of tackling distribution problems, however, needs to be flanked by action designed to improve farmers ability to achieve higher yields from their land—so they can feed themselves and others through their own efforts. If genetic engineering can help them do so and where it compares favourably to other options, so the use of GM plants should not be hindered.

If you look at the opportunities and risks GM might present for agriculture in developing countries. Pest-resistant Bt cotton, for example, has led to a marked upturn in yields in China and South Africa. In the South Africa province of Kwazulu/Natal, where the average farm is around 1.7 hectares small, the percentage of farmers who switched to genetically modified cotton from 1999 to 2002 jumped from 12 per cent to an estimated 95 per cent. One of the problems as sociated with Bt cotton is that 90 per cent of the biotech are held by a single enterprise—the Monsanto Group based in the USA. What's more, there are signs that resistance to cotton pests leads to an increase in other pests, which then need to be fought using more pesticides.

Taking a look at herbicide-resistant soya beans, the need to weigh up GM's pros and cons on a case by case basis. Herbicide resistance makes manual weeding unnecessary—which may be a handicap where desperately needed jobs could be lost. But where agriculture suffers from a growing shortage of labour—as it does in southern Africa due to AIDS-less labour-intensive crops could be a boon. However, in so-called "diversity centers" (region where many different varieties of a specific plant are grown)—such as Mexico (for maize) or India (for cotton)—the risk of non-GM crops being contaminated by air-borne pollen needs to be taken particularly seriously.

Among the prime requirements for the use of GM in agriculture are effective monitoring. Before introducing GM crops, the benefits and risks need to be carefully assessed. And after a permit is granted, care must be taken to ensure that farmers can buy seed at fair prices and have access to advice. In most developing countries, however, state institutions capable of providing such guarantees are few and far between. Such bodies need to be created, with the help of international development cooperation. In addition, developing countries have to cooperate more extensively at regional levels, for instance by sharing environmental impact assessments. The biotech companies operating in developing countries are called upon to involve smallscale farmers in their plant breeding operations so they can take greater account of their needs and preferences.

17

Migration and Development

Migration and development is a growing area of interest. There has been much debate on the negative impacts of migration on development and vice-versa. On the one hand, it is argued that underdevelopment is a cause of migration, and on the other that migration causes developing countries to lose their highly skilled nationals.

While there is a measure of truth in each of these assertions, properly managed international migration holds enormous potential for the development of countries. Remittances have become a prominent source of external funding for developing countries that surpass official development assistance. In 2005, over US $ 100 billion were sent home in remittances by migrants, helping to sustain the economies of many developing countries. The total amount of resource remitted may even be two or three times higher, since a large number of transactions are carried out through informal channels. Migration can thus contribute to the reduction of poverty at the local and national level, and to a reduction in the economic vulnerability of developing countries.

Migration may be detrimental to the community of origin if the labour market is depleted by the departure of its most productive and/or qualified members ("brain drain"). However, migrants who have developed and improved their skills abroad can be actors of the "brain gain" by transferring and infusing knowledge, skills and technology into their countries, of origin.

In addition, remittances sent home by migrants can be used to sustain development . The Challenge is to develop mechanisms to mitigate as much as possible the negative effects of "brain drain" and to encourage the return of qualified nationals resulting" brain gain"

It should also be noted that in a globalized world, migration is increasingly circular. While many migrants still make a permanent move with their families, an increasing proportion of migratory movements are temporary in nature. Increasingly, countries of origin expect migrants to maintain financial, cultural and sometimes political links with their home country, which may be difficult to reconcile with the expectation for migrants to integrate, on the part of the host country.

In order to benefit from remittances, skills transfer and investment opportunities, it is necessary to create and maintain links between migrants and their potential by encouraging them to contribute human and financial capital to the development of their home communities.

Through advances in communications technology and the decline in travel costs, globalization has made it easier for migrants to stay in contact with their country of origin and to establish lasting links with diasporas and transnational networks.

In the past, states and the international community formulated and implemented separate policies on poverty reduction, globalization, security, refugees and migration, with sometimes different or even conflicting objectives.

Better results can be achieved by considering the close interrelationship between migration and development on national and international levels through coherent and coordinated development and migration polices, and between humanitarian assistance and development assistance. Migration polices dealing with the migration—development nexus include facilitating voluntary return and reintegration, either temporary or permanent, particularly of the highly skilled. Other policies address the transfer of remittances, the reduction of transfer costs and investment in the country of origin by diasporas and returning migrants.

It is also necessary to promote and enhance dialogue and cooperation and the national level between different government agencies as well as at the international level. The aim is to ensure that migration contributes to sustainable development, and that in turn development endeavours to contribute to the management of migration.

In recent years, migration has been making its way steadily to the top of the international agenda, and now calls insistently and urgently for the attention of all governments, regard less of their past involvement or interest in the management of migratory processes.

Migratory flows today are more diverse and complex, with more temporary and circular migration. World demographics, economic, political and social trends mean that governments and societies will need to put more emphasis on migration management in all of its dimensions.

If properly managed, migration can be beneficial for all states and societies. If left unmanaged, it can lead to the exploitation of individual migrations, particularly through human trafficking and migrant smuggling, and be a source of social tension, insecurity and bad relations between nations.

Effective management is required to maximize the positive effects of migration and minimize potentially negative consequences. It is essential to establish orderly and safe migration opportunities while ensuring respect for the integrity of national, sovereign borders. Migration management strategies need to result in the implementation of policies; laws and regulations that take into account the rights and obligations of migrations as well as the social and economic interests of nations and responsibilities of governments.

Over the past decades governments have tended to focus on isolated elements of migration and have thus developed ad-hoc strategies to protect their interests. For some, labour migration needs have predominated, for others asylum has been the main concern. However, to be effective, migration management strategies need to address migration in a comprehensive manner. Governments over the past decades have tended to focus on isolated elements of migration. The challenge today is to shift from an isolate and largely in effective focus to more meaningful, constructive and comprehensive approaches.

At the same time, it is necessary to identify, define and address the fundamental policy issues in the migration debates. This is a tall. assignment, since the migratory landscape is complex and rapidly evolving, with challenges emerging at every step of the way.

Most governments are just beginning to develop coherent and comprehensive migration management strategies. There is still a need to better understand migration interests and priorities and to develop a common migration language. Regular dialogue between governments that allows an exchange of experience and the development of new initiatives and approaches to migration management is therefore essential.

18

The Trade Related Intellectual Property Rights (TRIPS) Agreement and the Developing Countries

The basic norms of free competition established in the nineteenth century induced legislators to provide relatively weak forms of intellectual property protection. Often innovators could rely only on such factors as lead time, reputation for quality and continuing technical improvements to maintain their foothold in the market.

Undermining this outlook were two developments that led to the inclusion of intellectual property issues in the World Trade Organisation (WTO). First, the rise of knowledge-based industries radically altered the nature of competition and disrupted the equilibrium that had resulted from more traditional comparative advantages. Second, the growing capacity of manufacturers in developing countries to penetrate distant markets for traditional industrial products forced the developed countries to rely more heavily on their comparative advantages in the production of intellectual goods than in the past. Market access for developing countries thus became a bargaining chip to be exchanged for greater protection of intellectual goods within a restructured global market place.

Since 1986 the developed countries' drive for extra-territorial protection of intellectual property rights has largely ignored the competitive capabilities of developing countries with respect to intellectual goods, and it has also downplayed these countries' rights to preferential treatment under existing rules. At the same time, the logic of multilateral trade negotiations skews the pre-existing North-South conflict over intellectual property rights by introducing the prospects of trade concessions in unrelated fields. Intellectual property rights constitute but one of many variables that bear on competitive capacity and the transfer of technology in general.

Primary Intellectual Property Regimes

Patents

The extension of patentability to virtually all types of technology recognised by developed patent systems, the prolongation of patent protection to a uniform term of twenty years, and legal recognition of the patentee's exclusive rights to import the relevant products could adversely affect developing countries whose existing patent laws fall below these standards. In practice, however, the competitive status of any given developing country in a post-TRIPS world will depend in part on the level of foreign direct investment it attracts and on the benefits that strengthened intellectual property rights bring to domestic innovators.

Competition under stronger patent regimes requires developing countries to adopt legal means of narrowing the scope of foreign patent monopolies and of encouraging local entrepreneurs either to work around the claimed inventions or to develop improvements suited to local conditions. To this end, local entrepreneurs should exploit technical information in disclosures published abroad; patent authorities should exercise all of the claims limitations practised abroad; and domestic courts should strictly interpret the doctrine of equivalents. Legislative enactments of utility model laws would provide additional incentives to adapt foreign inventions to local conditions and to improve them further.

Moreover, unpatented traditional technologies will often remain suitable for local needs, and the resulting products may be sold at lower prices than imported products of patented technologies. Entrepreneurs in developing countries should also be prepared to exploit unpatented applications of applied scientific know-how in such advanced technologies as biogenetic engineering and computer programme-related innovation.

In time, increased direct investment by foreign patentees could enable developing country licensees who exploit their natural advantages, especially low labour costs, to succeed on both domestic and export markets where non-licensees were unable or unwilling to venture in the past. Familiarisation with the benefits of the patent system should stimulate greater investment in domestic research and development and in technological innovation.

The gradual extension of patents to new technologies such as computer programmes and bio-genetic engineering without the emergence of agreed international minimum standards creates both opportunities and risks for the developing countries. While the developed countries enjoy unique advantages in biotechnology that only become available to developing countries as a consequence of stronger patent systems, some developing countries may find their own competitive status enhanced by the provision of proprietary rights, including plant breeders' rights, though others may not. The patenting of biogenetic advances decreases the scope for reverse-engineering and could also increase the costs of doing business in key sectors of some developing economies, notably agriculture. As regards information technologies, reliance on copyright and trade secrets at the international level appears less unfavourable to the developing countries' prospects than patents, for reasons that are set out below. However, the tendency to patent software could diminish these prospects by posing limits to reverse engineering and to the attainment of the interoperability, and this trend adds to the overall costs of disseminating information goods.

To the extent that patented technology is not made available on reasonable terms or that un-wholesome economic dependencies actually arise, developing countries will have to consider measures to restore the competitive balance that are consistent with the TRIPS agreement. For example, the agreement allows compulsory licences when the rights holders fail to licences patented technology "on reasonable commercial terms". It also provides other bases for defensive regulatory action by emphasising "the transfer and dissemination of technology, to the mutual advantage of producers and users" and the need "to promote the public interest in sectors of vital importance to socio-economic and technological development".

Measures to restrain abuses of intellectual property rights as authorised by the Paris Convention also remain available under the TRIPS agreement, which expressly empowers developing countries to deal with licensing practices that "adversely affect the international transfer of technology".

Finally, the agreement specifically preserves the right of all states to "adopt measures necessary to protect public health and nutrition and to promote the public interest in sectors of vital importance to socio-economic and technological development, provided that such measures are consistent with the provisions of this agreement".

Trademarks and Geographical Indications

The TRIPS provisions give pre-existing norms greater specificity while softening the use requirement and eliminating both compulsory licences and local linkage requirements. These provisions also subject the international regime of trade marks and unfair competition to more stringent enforcement measures, including border controls against imports of counterfeit goods.

As a result, developing countries will need to reassess the pro-competitive functions of trade marks in open economies while addressing questions of abuse in a more direct fashion. They should insist on receiving the technical cooperation and aid that the TRIPS agreement envisages for the purpose of defraying administrative and enforcement burdens.

Governments should consider policies and incentives that encourage enterprises to establish their own market identities through appropriate trade marks and foreign firms to allow licensees to adapt more of the licenced products for both domestic and export needs under local trade marks.

Copyrights

Authors in many developing countries are very active in both domestic and foreign markets. It nonetheless remains true that the balance of trade in cultural goods favours exports from developed countries. This imbalance could increase under the TRIPS agreement, which generally applies the international minimum standards of the Berne Convention, plus selected standards from the Rome Convention on neighbouring rights.

While efforts to implement these standards is mandatory, developing country authorities should familiarise themselves with the extent to which the scope of copyright protection varies from country to country, in the absence of authoritative legal limitations recognised by international law. Carefully framed public-interest exceptions may further reduce the overall costs of a TRIPS agreement without violating international copyright norms. Moreover, the revised Berne Convention already provides for compulsory licences for educational and scientific test, and developing countries may wish to consider making greater use of these concessions.

Ancillary Proprietary Regimes

Trade Secrets

In modern economies trade secret law regulates the pace of competition by endowing second comers with an absolute right to reverse-engineer. To operate successfully under such a regime, developing countries must realign the concept of "transfer of technology" with the nature of competition on open markets. Technology is transferred through self-help methods of reverse engineering. The potential benefits of reverse-engineering unpatented technologies increase when advanced technologies are involved, notably biogenetic engineering, computer programmes and computer-aided design. The unpatented, non-copyrightable know-how underlying these technologies is often embodied in tangible products available to the pubic, which renders classical trade secret protection of doubtful efficacy. By ignoring this problem, the TRIPS Agreement provides entrepreneurs in developing countries with major opportunities, notwithstanding the extension of trade secret law under TRIPS, provided they are willing and able to master the art of reverse-engineering.

Other Proprietary Regimes

The TRIPS Agreement mandates intellectual property protection for industrial designs, plant varieties and integrated circuit designs. Although the developed countries enjoy a clear advantage in advanced sectors of industrial design, more traditional sectors rooted in aesthetic appeal rather than technical efficiency remain accessible to firms in developing countries.

Need for Multilateral Policies

Global economic integration increasingly requires that intangible creations receive minimum international standards of legal protection. Purely territorial intellectual property rights will thus give way to international sovereignty. However, the norms, of that law represent a delicate balance between the interests of States at different stages of development, so that the evolution of international intellectual property law will have to accommodate these norms and that balance.

Efforts to implement higher intellectual property standards will put increasing strains on competition law, which is not directly covered by the TRIPS Agreement. Identifying the parameters of healthy competition valid for all players in an integrated world market will become a pressing task for the international community in a post-TRIPS world. These issues will be complicated by the fact that innovators, users, and second comers all have different stakes in fashioning the rules of unfair competition law, and their interests will increasingly vary more with their economic roles than with the geopolitical affiliations of their respective national States.

Competition law must, become an integral part of international discussions of intellectual property rights, and there is a great need for multilateral cooperation to achieve a marketwide balance between incentives to create, and reasonable opportunities to imitate and improve upon, technological innovation. These discussions should lead to an internationally agreed framework for promoting a transfer of technology that is compatible with the drive for greater economic efficiency. To the extent that such cooperation succeeds, it will contribute a new perspective to the notion of fair competition that should strengthen the prospects of all participants in the global marketplace.

19

Helping Your Child Learn

A one-syllable word begins the education process: "Why?" Parents are always trying to answer that question. And that interaction between parent and child is the basis of much that children learn.

Teaching and learning are not mysteries that can happen only in school. They can also happen when parents and children do simple things together—things such as:

- Figure out whose socks are whose-sorting is a major function in maths and science;
- Cook a meal to learn science and good health;
- Tell each other a story as an important beginning for reading and writing; if the story is about the past, it's a way to interest a child in history;
- Plan a visit to a friend or relative for a personal connection with geography;
- Or play a game of hopscotch to develop counting and lifelong fitness;
- All children love their friends. So ask your child to describe his friend's appearance at the end of each school day. You can ask questions like. "What outfit did he/she wear?" or "How did he/she do his/her hair? This kind of routine query would encourage your child to observe his friend more minutely;

- If your child goes to school by bus, he can be asked to describe his route and point out certain landmarks namely colourful posters, traffic signals, large shops etc.

By doing things with their children, parents show that learning is fun and important—and that encourages children to study, learn, and stay in school.

Even on the discipline front, parents can help their children. Basic disciplinary principles must be tailored to each child and family. Before parents can become effective disciplinarians, they must first learn how to manage their own anger, solve problem situations and give and get support from others. Simple self-help techniques with or without professional support can help parents sharply reduce discipline problems.

Parents who are sensitive to their children's needs have more obedient children. Praise and love alone are not enough to instil good behaviour. Too much permissiveness hurts a child's efforts to develop self-control.

Behaviour problems should be reversed early. Waiting until the preteen-age years diminishes chances for success and puts children at higher risk for drug use and other problems.

Parents need to learn as many tricks of the trade as possible, including how to play with their children, communicate with them, praise and reward them and also set limits for them, as well as how to handle misbehaviour using a variety of techniques.

All that parents need to help their children is a willingness to observe and learn with them, and, to take the time to nurture their natural curiosity.

❍ ❍ ❍

20

Aid Effectiveness as a Multi-level Process

Parallel to the widespread decrease of aid resources provided by donor countries to developing countries in recent years, debate and research on how to make aid more effective has become a major concern. Usually, it is suggested that decades of development assistance have at best produced marginal results in terms of improving development levels in the South. Little mention is made of donor's policy shortcomings and the negative impact of these on efforts aimed at reforming and redefining development cooperation in order to enhance aid effectiveness. The policy parameters and operating frameworks of existing aid policies continue to inhibit higher degrees of aid effectiveness. In many donor countries, opinion polls indicate waning public support for development aid.

Increasingly, the moral case for aid is called into question and deeper world market integration tends to be seen as the panacea to continued economic decline and social destabilisation in the South. Against this background, cooperation between donor and recipient actors is faced with a duel uphill struggle. First, fewer resources can be mobilised to meet growing developmental needs. On the other hand, to organise and manage development policies and programmes in a result-oriented manner, grows more difficult. The threat of further aid cuts and of further drops of public support for providing aid become ever more real. A closer look at the organisational complexities and political constraints under which development cooperation is expected to perform effectively may help to improve current aid management approaches.

Towards Conceptual Clarity

At first, catchy definitions of what constitutes effective aid might appear attractive to use, in particular with regard to economic indicators. The term "aid effectiveness" is easily used in the same vein as "efficiency", "significance" or "impact" of aid. At times, obsession to measure and demonstrate the results of aid supported development processes can be observed among policy-makers and administrators on the donor side. Still the understanding of aid and its effectiveness as being part and parcel of a cooperation relationship between donor and recipient side parties, is scarcely embedded in practice. To determine how to make aid more effective requires more than a quick impact analysis of an individual and perhaps even isolated development project. Consequently, defining the concept of aid effectiveness needs to take into account at what levels cooperation is focused on. To strive for sustainable and effective modes of development cooperation will entail the need to combine recipient ownership of the development process with donor accountability concerns.

Performance expectations cannot be exclusively placed on the recipient while donor interests, their aid management systems and procedures remain unchanged.

An extended and more analytical, process-oriented definition should take into account four main aspects of aid effectiveness:

(a) Effective aid must relate to the building and/or strengthening of in-country aid management capacity;

(b) To maximise the degree of aid effectiveness, local ownership of the aid process is essential: from setting of priorities through policy formulation and implementation on to the evaluation stages of the process;

(c) Increasing recipient side capabilities to take charge of aid relationship, will need to be combined with arrangements to meet legitimate donor accountability concerns;

(d) Aid effectiveness is a two-faceted objective: its realisation is equally dependent on increased transparency of donor motives and on dropping of non-developmental, political and economic aid objectiveness of donors.

In addition a broader range of stakeholders in the aid relationship needs to be actively involved: extending beyond accountable government and implementing agencies, to include democratic institutions and organisations of civil society and of the private sector.

Applying any definition of aid effectiveness without disaggregating macro-economic data and taking into account country specificity will only lead to unhelpful generalisations about aid and its effectiveness. It would seem more appropriate to adopt working definitions against which to assess effectiveness of aid resources at a country-specific level. On such a basis one could expect to arrive at more reliable indicators of how well aid resources contribute to improving developmental standards and meeting existing needs.

From Definition to Success—Key Requirements

Having reached agreement between the recipient and donor on what should constitute effectiveness of aid is only a starting point. Embarking on democratic, peaceful and participatory patterns of economic and social development must follow: to arrive at significant and lasting improvement in many of the least developed countries will be a long-term process. This being said, it is crucial to design and implements such forms of development cooperation which involve a wide range of recipient side actors, not only from the government side but also from civil society at large. Seen as a process of increasing inclusion of intended beneficiaries of aid, the commitment to decentralise as well as entrust aid and its management grows in importance.

To fully capture Third World development realities, policy frameworks inspired by neoliberalist-type of development concepts and theories are grossly inadequate. The views and positions on aid articulated in the World Bank and the IMF, and others, represent only one side of today's international cooperation, namely the donor side. The major weakness to point out with respect to this locus of debate, is a profound under representation if not even a total absence of recipient experiences and perceptions on aid in general and on its effectiveness in particular. There should be little doubt that ignoring to not actively identifying and involving such perceptions, leads to strongly donor driven aid.

To circumvent recipient side insights and views on strengths and weaknesses of aid strategies and mechanisms, will result in limited local commitment and sense of ownership over the aid process. Mutual decision-making between donors and recipients remains a rare policy approach. Aid procedures that are based on local management and less control-oriented donor roles in the aid process are still exceptions in development cooperation.

Structurally, in terms of the policy environment within which development aid is expected to function, the overriding policy framework is generally based on structural adjustment policies (SAP). But the underlying conclusion made by proponents of SAPs that these policies induce aid effectiveness, has yet to be proven valid. It must suffice at this point to emphasize that there is no *a priori* relationship between world market integration under structural adjustment and sustainable development in poor countries. Aid to these countries which is solely intended to reinforce fundamentally uneven and unequal patterns of world market integration should be scrutinised critically.

Some central issues need to be addressed in the course of improving aid and its effectiveness:

- institutional dimensions of aid relationships require strong policy-attention, both on the donor and the recipient side;
- capacities to effectively identify and formulate aid priorities need to be strengthened in recipient countries;
- local capacities to sustain reform efforts must be reinforced.

Levels of Intervention

If the design of aid and the terms upon which it is provided to a developing country are largely determined by the donor, the aid relationship can be characterised as essentially hierarchical. Recipient side views will rarely surface, as they are either not identified, or not well formulated. Possibilities of a recipient-led development strategies can be limited. Unless scope is provided to the recipient side actors to assume responsibilities, aid effectiveness is likely to remain low or fluctuating, and the sustainability of donor aid efforts will remain doubtful.

National planning processes and courses of national development in recipient countries should be seen as most effective where they are led under local responsibility and control. To arrive at this ideal situation, gaps need to be reduced and closed at the various intervention levels.

Donor aid resources provide valuable support for this process. Their effectiveness in meeting long-term objective of aid will need to be assessed on the basis of how well they perform at the different levels. Individual donors will expectedly perform differently at the various levels. What will prove to be the ultimate test for effectiveness is how well the donor aid performance accomplishes the broader objectives of development cooperation and how well it includes sustainable results.

In the analytical frameworks outlined here, development cooperation would seem to be confronted with the effectiveness gaps at the:

- *Structural Level:* International trade and investment patterns, debt problems and world market integration process appear as long-term constraining factors upon aid and its effectiveness;
- *Policy Level:* Dialogue and partnership in development cooperation are instrumental factors in recluding planning and co-ordination gaps with regard to policy analysis and formulation;
- *The Institutional Level* is where pertinent capacity gaps exist: capacity development efforts of donors and technical assistance measures play an important role in addressing weaknesses in aid effectiveness within a country's institutional setting;
- Finally, at the *level of aid projects* (programmes), it is generally the lack of sustainability of aid interventions which causes development activities to falter once donor support decreases or stops. In addition to technical cooperation, financial and material inputs serve to maintain project momentum and goal realisation. The issue of how to develop local capacity sufficiently in order for indigenous organisations to continue project activities initially supported by donor aid, remains the most important issue to address at this level.

Fostering Aid Effectiveness

In recent years donor aid budgets have been reshuffled, while having decreased in real terms. Geographical redistributions of reduced aid budgets have been accompanied by the need to accommodate rising emergency needs.

Additional resources to meet these needs have not been forthcoming: in general, aid budgets destined for developmental purposes have been under severe pressures while urgent humanitarian needs have added to the drain on resources.

Donor and recipient development efforts are too often isolated from one another, or poorly coordianted. They fail to address managerial and implementation bottlenecks. Cross-sectoral linkages, as well as interdisciplinary approaches to aid problems are only slowly gaining ground. It is increasingly obvious, that decisions on aid issues are subjected to concerns outside of the responsible ministry: Finance Ministers, Economic Ministers, and unfortunately even Defence Ministers have a strong say in how much aid is to be provided, where it is to be concentrated and under what terms to be utilised. Inside of recipient countries, large portions of national budgets are allocated to non-development priorities with little or no impact on alleviating urgent poverty problems.

Development cooperation may make the biggest impact and be executed most effectively where donors and recipients agree upon multi-level aid strategies. To give an example, building a road to a remote rural area may well be done in an effective project manner. It is equally important to have a functioning transport authority in place to ensure maintenance of the roads. If this authority operates within a nationally defined infrastructure policy, best in accord with national trade and investment priorities, then the effectiveness of the project-level road building programme has a good chance of being high.

Institutional changes to set the stage for a profound reform process in development cooperation are needed. Reprioritising national budgets to reflect identified in country development needs may be one step. Setting up policy evaluation and formulation units can be complimentary measures. Deregulating markets and investment rules may serve to please donors, but dumping of cheap products which strangle local production efforts may easily result. Regional cooperation, including intensified

South-South cooperation can provide some counterbalance. There are only a few areas where changes in the current system of development cooperation can occur, with a view to better manage the complexities of aid and the social, cultural, economic and political backgrounds against which they take place. The will and commitment to take policy action in both donor and recipient countries, through the broadest range of stakeholders and institutions as possible, will be the test for genuine efforts at improving development relations between North and South and organising cooperation effectively.

Bibliography

Anand, R.P., *Legal Regime of Sea Bed and the Developing Countries,* 1975.

Bhatt, S., *Environment Protection and International Law,* Radiant Publication, Kalkaji, New Delhi, 1985, p. 122.

Bhatt, S., *Environmental Laws and Water Resources Management,* Radiant Publication, India, and Advent Books Inc., New York, 1986, p. 355.

Behrman, Danial, *In Partnership with Nature—UNESCO and the Environment,* Paris, 1973.

Bell, Daniel, "Technology, Nature and Society", *American Scholar,* Summer, 1973.

Bentley, Glass, Biology and Human Values, USIS, New Delhi.

Book of Nature. The Way Things Work, George Allen and Unwin Ltd., 1981, p. 525.

Boulding, Kenneth E., New Goals for Society, S.H. Schun, ed., *Energy, Economic Growth and the Environment.*

Carr, E.H., *What is History,* 1961.

Darlington, C.D., *The Evolution of Man and Society,* London, 1961.

Downing, Paul B., ed., *Air Pollution and Social Sciences,* New York, 1971.

"Drive to Adopt National Water Policy", *Times of India,* 22 July 1983.

Dubos, Rene, "Man and His Environment", *Britannica Perspectives,* Vol. 1, 1968.

Einstein, A., *My Views,* ed., by S.K. Bandopadhyaya, Calcutta, 1976.

Environment Research Programme, Prepared by NCEPC, Department of Science and Technology, New Delhi.

Forbes, R.J., "The Conquest of Nature and Its Consequences", *Britannica Perspectives,* Vol. 1, 1968.

Fowler, John M., *Energy and Environment,* New York, 1975.

Fuller, Buckminister, R., *Operating Manual for Spaceship Earth,* New York, 1969.

Gandhi, Indira, "Poverty Greatest Pollution, says Mrs. Gandhi", *Times of India,* 8 September 1981.

Glenn, Seaborg, "Science, Technology and Development: A New World Outlook", USIS, New Delhi.

Hacoley, Amos H., *Human Ecology,* New York, 1950.

"India Must Develop Own Ecology", *Times of India,* 8 October 1981.

Marion, Jerry B., *Energy in Perspective,* London, 1974.

Misra, K.C., *Manual of Plant Ecology,* New Delhi, 1980.

Mukherji, P.K., *Life of Tagore,* translate, by S.K. Ghosh, 1975.

Mumford, Lewis, "The Future of Cities", in *Basic Issues in Environment,* E.J. Winn, ed., 1972.

Palmslierna, H., *Future Imperatives for Human Environment,* 1972.

Pavithran, A.K., "World Futurology", *Eastern Journal of International Law,* Madras, Vol. 9.

"Plans to Usher India into 21st Century", *Times of India,* 24 October 1985.

Polunin, Nicholas, "The Biosphere Today", *The Environmental Future,* Proceedings of 1st International Conference on Environmental Future in Finland, ed. by N. Polunin, 1972.

Radhakrishnan, S., *Recovery of Faith,* 1967.

Report on the State of Environment, prepared by Centre for Science and Environment, New Delhi, 1985.

Sarkar, Mahendra Nath, *The Cultural Heritage of India,* Vol. 1.

Sen, Sudhir, "Blueprint for a Better World", *Times of India,* 2 March 1980.

The Limits to Growth, A Report to Club of Rome, New York, 1972.

The Mind of J. Krishnamurti, ed. by L.S.R. Vas, Bombay, 1971.

Toynbee, Arnold, "Man and His Soul", *Hindustan Times,* 4 January 1968.

United Nations List of National Parks and Protected Areas, 1985.

Vivekananda, Swami, *Complete Works,* Vol. II, Calcutta, 1968.

Ward, Barbara and Dubos Rene, *Only One Earth: The Care and Maintenance of a Small Planet,* Report to UN Conference on Human Environment, Stockholm, 1972.

"Wildlife Laws in India", *Times of India,* 4 March 1985.

Ward, Barbara, *Progress for a Small Planet,* 1979.

Index